Coaching Education Leaders

This exciting book is designed to help coaches, or individuals in a coaching and/or capacity-building role, support educators in becoming culturally responsive leaders. *Coaching Education Leaders* describes a unique *Facilitative Competency-Based Coaching* approach formulated by the nationally recognized nonprofit organization The Leadership Academy. Using six *Equity Leadership Dispositions* as its foundation, this model helps educators identify and directly address inequities in their schools to ensure the academic, social, and emotional success of all students. The strategies in this book help coaches plan the full arc of the coaching experience, from identifying goals and assessing progress, to designing each session to meet the individual learning needs of their coachees. To bring these coaching ideas to life, this book shares real stories from the field, illustrating the coach-leader relationship and takeaway tools for readers to immediately apply in their own work. The authors share practical coaching techniques to create a safe learning space and engage coachees in the deeper levels of dialogue required to identify and address systems-level adaptive challenges. This self-paced guide to coaching educators is a key resource for anyone interested in developing others' for the sake of creating meaningful and sustainable change in their schools, school systems, and in the leaders who lead both.

Nancy B. Gutiérrez is President and Lead Executive Officer of The Leadership Academy, USA.

Michelle Jarney is Executive Director of Learning and Strategy at The Leadership Academy, USA.

Michael Kim is the lead for national coaching services at The Leadership Academy, USA and the Senior Director of Leadership Development.

"*Coaching Education Leaders* is an invaluable resource to guide coaches who strive to develop equitable and culturally responsive school and system leaders. It provides proven guideposts for growing leaders who can create safe and inclusive schools and enable the high-quality teaching that is essential for our nation's students to learn deeply and thrive in today's world."

Linda Darling-Hammond, *President, Learning Policy Institute and Professor Emeritus, Stanford University, USA*

"The Leadership Academy's *Coaching Education Leaders* is an important book for our time and profession. Every school leadership coach can learn powerful and explicit ways to build the capacity of school and systems leaders to create more equitable schools."

Gary Bloom, *Former Superintendent, Santa Cruz City Schools & Co-Founder, New Teacher Center, USA*

"I became hooked on the profound impact of facilitative coaching when The Leadership Academy trained me as a coach in Delaware many years ago. I've been using this approach ever since. *Coaching Education Leaders* is an indispensable resource that should be in every coach's toolkit."

Jackie Owens Wilson, Ed.D., *Executive Director, National Policy Board for Educational Administration, USA*

"Every leader dedicated to truly advancing educational and economic advancement for communities of color needs a coach who adopts a facilitative approach. Gutiérrez, Jarney, and Kim's book offers indispensable tools and techniques to help coaches guide leaders to reach their learning edge and make a profound difference in the lives of all students, and especially students of color."

Sharhonda Bossier, *CEO, Education Leaders of Color, USA*

"My coach from The Leadership Academy has guided my professional and personal growth for the past 16 years, from school principal to district superintendent. The *facilitative coaching* approach helped me peel back the layers in my and others' mental models about student achievement and allows me to share my full self as an Asian American immigrant system leader striving to close the knowing-doing gap. This is a must-have reference book for every coach!"

Hoa Tu, Ed.D., *Superintendent, Queens North High Schools, NYC Public Schools, USA*

"Breakthroughs occur when leaders effectively turn obstacles into opportunities. The secret to that lies in having a coach who provides critical questions, thought partnership, and responsive feedback. In this book, The Leadership Academy shares its decades of invaluable insights and tools to unleash the power of coaching for both leader and organizational success."

Ruby Ababio-Fernandez, Ed.D., *Executive Vice President, Courageous, USA*

"We need more educators who are not afraid to take bold steps to emancipate those who were not part of the initial schema of education. *Coaching Education Leaders* is a must-read primer for all coaches who are passionate about building courageous leaders that disrupt today's context."

Edward Fergus Arcia, Ph.D., *Professor of Urban Education and Policy, Rutgers University-Newark, USA*

"The Leadership Academy's facilitative approach is exactly the type of coaching that research tells us is the most impactful professional learning for principals. This book provides practical tools to develop high-quality coaches who build the capacity of school and system leaders to advance achievement for all students."

Rotunda Floyd-Cooper, Ed.D., *Vice President, Education Leadership, The Wallace Foundation, USA*

"All school leaders will benefit from learning how to be facilitative coaches. The Leadership Academy has successfully been developing principals for years. Their equity based coaching approach is no longer a choice; it is a must. This book makes it available to us all!"

Janet Patti, Ed.D., *Professor Emeritus, Hunter College, USA*

"I am the leader I am today thanks to the invaluable support of my Leadership Academy experience and leadership coach. With *Coaching Education Leaders*, every coach and every leader in the system can benefit from the transformative facilitative competency-based approach to coaching that used to be available only to a privileged few."

Danika Rux, Ed.D., *Deputy Chancellor, Division of School Leadership, NYCPS, USA*

"Building the capacity of others is core to effective leadership. As a leader in an urban district and now a state leader, I found this approach to coaching invaluable in helping confront our biases and giving us the courage to break the historical patterns of inequity that have resulted in far too few black, brown and low-income children succeeding at high levels. Our leaders grew their ability to talk about the real barriers and support their teams to drive achievement for all kids."

Susana Córdova, *Colorado Commissioner of Education, USA*

"Anyone who wants to be a better coach to school leaders will find this book a gift that keeps on giving! Great coaching begins with empathy – and really effective empathy requires both feeling and accurate understanding. What makes *Coaching Education Leaders* such a valuable resource is its interest in helping the coach to open both heart and mind."

Robert Kegan, Ph.D, *Meehan Professor Emeritus, Harvard Graduate School of Education, USA*

"Every school leader needs an effective coach to support them in creating the positive and safe environment that is vital to ensure that all young people are able to achieve their full potential. Gutiérrez, Jarney, and Kim's book offers an invaluable approach to coach school leaders to lead schools that help close opportunity gaps and equip all students for success."

John B. King, Jr., *Chancellor, The State University of New York, and former US Secretary of Education, USA*

Other Eye on Education Books Available from Routledge
(www.routledge.com/eyeoneducation)

A Leadership Playbook for Addressing Rapid Change in Education: Empowered for Success
Teresa L. San Martín

Improving Teacher Morale and Motivation: Leadership Strategies that Build Student Success
Ronald Williamson and Barbara R. Blackburn

Lead with Truth: How to Make a Difference in Your School, Your Life, and the Lives of Your Students
Qiana O'Leary

When Black Students Excel: How Schools Can Engage and Empower Black Students
Joseph F. Johnson, Jr., Cynthia L. Uline, and Stanley J. Munro, Jr.

Mismeasuring Schools' Vital Signs
Steve Rees and Jill Wynns

First Aid for Teacher Burnout: How You Can Find Peace and Success, 2nd Edition
Jenny Grant Rankin

Leading School Culture through Teacher Voice and Agency
Sally J. Zepeda, Philip D. Lanoue, David R. Shafer, Grant M. Rivera

Becoming an International School Educator: Stories, Tips, and Insights from Teachers and Leaders
Edited by Dana Specker Watts and Jayson W. Richardson

The Principal's Desk Reference to Professional Standards: Actionable Strategies for Your Practice
Robyn Conrad Hansen and Frank D. Davidson

Trailblazers for Whole School Sustainability: Case Studies of Educators in Action
Cynthia L. Merse, Jennifer Seydel, Lisa A.W. Kensler, and David Sobel

Get Organized Digitally!: The Educator's Guide to Time Management
Frank Buck

The Confident School Leader: 7 Keys to Influence and Implement Change
Kara Knight

Coaching Education Leaders: A Culturally Responsive Approach to Transforming Schools and Systems
Nancy B. Gutiérrez, Michelle, Jarney, and Michael Kim

Coaching Education Leaders
A Culturally Responsive Approach to Transforming Schools and Systems

Nancy B. Gutiérrez,
Michelle Jarney, and Michael Kim

Designed cover image: © Getty Images

First published 2025
by Routledge
605 Third Avenue, New York, NY 10158

and by Routledge
4 Park Square, Milton Park, Abingdon, Oxon, OX14 4RN

Routledge is an imprint of the Taylor & Francis Group, an informa business

© 2025 The Leadership Academy

The right of The Leadership Academy to be identified as author of this work has been asserted in accordance with sections 77 and 78 of the Copyright, Designs and Patents Act 1988.

All rights reserved. No part of this book may be reprinted or reproduced or utilised in any form or by any electronic, mechanical, or other means, now known or hereafter invented, including photocopying and recording, or in any information storage or retrieval system, without permission in writing from the publishers.

Trademark notice: Product or corporate names may be trademarks or registered trademarks, and are used only for identification and explanation without intent to infringe.

ISBN: 978-0-367-43618-6 (hbk)
ISBN: 978-0-367-81930-9 (pbk)
ISBN: 978-1-003-01087-6 (ebk)

DOI: 10.4324/9781003010876

Typeset in Warnock Pro
by SPi Technologies India Pvt Ltd (Straive)

Coaching Education Leaders is dedicated to everyone who is committed to coaching school and system leaders to become the best version of themselves and to transform education on behalf of students.

Contents

Foreword	*xv*
Preface	*xviii*
Acknowledgments	*xix*
Meet the Authors	*xxi*

Introduction   1

▶ **Chapter 1**   Unpacking Facilitative Competency-Based Coaching   11

▶ **Chapter 2**   Centering Equity in Leadership Coaching   28

▶ **Chapter 3**   Initiating the Coaching Relationship   50

▶ **Chapter 4**   Creating the Conditions to Go Deep   68

▶ **Chapter 5**   Bringing Your Coachee to the Learning Edge   89

▶ **Chapter 6**   Maximizing Impact in Practical Ways   109

Conclusion   124

Appendix A: Equity Leadership Instrument Excerpt for Reference Only — *126*

Appendix B: Goal-Setting Workbook — *130*

Appendix C: Additional Questions Corresponding to Clutterbuck's Levels of Dialogue — *134*

Appendix D: Excerpt of The Leadership Academy's Portrait of a Classroom: A Culturally and Linguistically Responsive Walkthrough Guide — *138*

Appendix E: School Level "Iceberg" Diagnostic Process — *148*

Glossary — *155*

Foreword

When I first became a school principal, my supervisor coached, guided, and helped me sharpen my leadership skills to better serve all students. She gave me consistent feedback and was always there to lend a supportive ear and push me to take risks. She asked probing questions. She helped me clarify my values, learn about myself, and consider problems from different angles. Even though she was technically my supervisor and evaluator, every moment was an opportunity for growth and learning. She honored her responsibility as a capacity builder – a *coach*.

Like *Facilitative Competency-Based (FCB) Coaching*, her questions were pointed but open-ended. Some were technical. "What are your backup plans?" But, most questions were adaptive and focused on strategy. "How will you cultivate student and teacher ownership? How will you launch your literacy work?" Many explored my beliefs, emotions, ideas, and actions. "What do you need to do differently to make your vision come to life? What's stopping you from acting more boldly? What are you afraid of?" Her questions almost always came back to my impact on students and educational equity. "Who are you helping the most with that decision? And who might it hinder?"

From strategy conversations to dialogue that focused on my personal beliefs about children, my supervisor used coaching to bring out my best. She cultivated a relationship with me, so I was more receptive to feedback and open to greater growth. Her reflective listening and thoughtful questioning led to personal insights and changes in my behavior, even when the answers were uncomfortable. Because of her, I now consistently consider the costs and benefits of a potential plan, and I analyze the unintended consequences of different options before I choose a course of action. I owe much of my leadership to her skillful coaching.

Seventeen years later, I can still hear some of her questions and guidance in my head as I navigate new situations and make difficult leadership decisions. Her greatest gift to me was how she helped me reframe my role as an education leader. I wasn't just the school disciplinarian or purveyor of resources. She helped me see myself as a developer of adult learners. *Growing adults to grow students* became my mantra, and it has guided me in my career ever since as a principal, as a leadership coach, and as the former vice president of leadership coaching for The Leadership Academy and the lead designer of our coaching model refresh. Through interviews, field observations, analysis of practice, and research, I worked with Michael Kim, Michelle Jarney, and the organization's coaches to develop our coaching competencies while honoring the core of the original FCB Model.

With this book, The Leadership Academy invites you to use coaching to develop others and take up the mantra of *growing adults to grow students.*

- Are you a leader looking to adopt a coaching stance with the people you supervise and support?
- Are you seeking ways to center equity in your coaching conversations and move beyond discussing scheduling, observations, and other mundane matters?
- Do you need help balancing accountability with support?

The Leadership Academy has developed and refined the answers to these questions over the course of 20 years, and in this book, the authors share The Leadership Academy's proven approach and hard-earned experience coaching and growing leaders across the nation. Whether you coach formally or serve as an informal coach, have one year of experience or a decade, this book can help you learn new concepts and techniques to spark meaningful and lasting leadership change through The Leadership Academy's signature coaching model: FCB Coaching. Each chapter also includes real coaching scenarios to help you envision coaching tools in action and what considerations to keep in mind as you adopt a coaching stance.

I use FCB Coaching and the tools in this book on a regular basis in my current work. I am a father now, and after my daughter was born, I went back to the best job in the world – leading a school. In the same way my supervisor once coached me, as a principal, I now coach my assistant principals and teacher leaders. Through coaching, we explore the potential impact of decisions. We strengthen curriculum and ensure all students see positive representations of themselves in our books, on our walls, and in our faculty. We explore our beliefs and the extent to which our actions are in alignment with them. Through coaching, we hone our communication skills to better engage and partner with parents, and we consistently ask ourselves what are the intended and unintended consequences of each choice before us.

I hope this book becomes a treasured resource for you as you seek to become a better coach and make a meaningful difference in students' lives. Capture your reflections after each chapter. Earmark passages so you can go back to them and scribble your thoughts in the margins. Whatever your style, use the information. Use it to start a new coaching relationship or deepen an existing one. Leverage the FCB Coaching Model and questioning strategies to elevate your current practice and give educational equity greater prominence in your work. Talk about it with colleagues so you can advance a shared vision of leadership development and growth on behalf of students, especially those who need us most. Most importantly, join The Leadership Academy in the hard work of leadership growth and transformation so that one day, every system can have a great leader and every child can have a school where they matter, are seen, appreciated, and can thrive.

Francis Yasharian, Ed.L.D

Preface

The Leadership Academy is a nationally recognized nonprofit organization with a clear mission: to build the capacity of educational leaders at every level of the system, to confront inequities, and to create the conditions necessary for all students to thrive. Since our founding in 2003, we have worked with nearly 14,000 school and system leaders, helping 11.5 million students learn in schools with stronger leadership. Our current reach extends across 40 states and more than 430 school systems. When compared to the national average, the typical districts we support serve significantly more: students of color; multilingual students; neurodiverse students; and students who live in poverty.

We know that sustainable, systemic change takes strategic support, strong commitment, and new ways of engaging with students, families, and teachers. This is why we work side-by-side with partner school systems to ensure local teams are prepared to build on and sustain the work long after our collaboration with them has ended. We:

- Provide professional learning, coaching, and strategic consulting for school and system leaders to develop and sustain culturally responsive leadership.
- Partner with leaders to build system-level capacity to address inequities and design exceptional learning opportunities for every student.
- Create leadership pathways that ensure diversification of leadership across the system from the classroom to the superintendency.

Over the past 20 years, we have sharpened our focus on the "how" of dismantling systemic inequities in schools: culturally responsive leadership. The FCB Coaching approach you find in this book incorporates the research, practice, and contributions of many coaches and staff, all dedicated to developing great leaders who can tap into educators' capacity to unleash the powers of young people.

Acknowledgments

In developing our approach, The Leadership Academy leveraged coaching models such as Gary Bloom's and Jackie Wilson's work on *Blended Coaching*, which addresses issues of professional practice and social and emotional dispositions and skills, Elena Aguilar's social-emotional-oriented transformative model, and Robert Kegan and Lisa Lahey's Immunity to Change Model, which addresses the competing priorities that arise when we seek to change behaviors. Senge's work on systems thinking undergirds our beliefs about organizational change. Gloria Ladson-Billings and Zaretta Hammond have been influential in our thinking around culturally responsive education and leadership. The work of The Wallace Foundation on school leadership, Eddie Fergus on addressing disproportionality, and Linda Darling-Hammond on developing effective principals and instructional leadership for systemic change has laid a foundation for our practice. All these thought leaders have helped inform The Leadership Academy's FCB Coaching approach.

This book was founded on the brilliance of The Leadership Academy's current and former coaches, staff, and leaders. We particularly want to acknowledge Sandra Stein, Claire McIntee, and Francis Yasharian, who each played a pivotal role in defining, shaping, and growing FCB Coaching, as well as the invaluable contributions of prior CEOs and organization leaders, including Irma Zardoya, Kathy Nadurak, Courtney Welsh, and Bob Knowling. Gratitude to our board of directors, with special thanks to our board chair, Jonathan Moses. We also want to honor all of The Leadership Academy coaches – past and present – who brought this practice to life over the last two decades and give special thanks to Sonia Bu, Liliana Polo-McKenna, Mary Rice-Boothe, David Baiz, Anthony King, Anthony Alston, Kathy Elliot, Karen Maldonado, Sharon Bonifazio, Annalise Kontras, and Sarah Stevens-Malcolm, who each shared their stories and perspectives over innumerable interviews. We owe a debt of gratitude to the many people whose organizational and editorial support made this book possible, including Mary Jo Dunnington, Carole Learned-Miller, Marianna Fischer, Juanita Lewis, Nikki Nagler, Jill Grossman, Erica Van Ross, Lorene Sachwald, and Aiesha Eleusizov. Finally, special thanks to our founders, partners, funders, advisors, long-time friends and alumni – too many to name – whose partnership and advocacy have empowered us to create and innovate for so many years.

Meet the Authors

▶ **Nancy B. Gutiérrez** is President and Lead Executive Officer of The Leadership Academy, a nationally recognized nonprofit organization dedicated to supporting and developing culturally responsive school and school system leaders to create the conditions necessary for all students to thrive. Prior to joining The Leadership Academy, Nancy launched and led a New York City Department of Education program for executive leadership advancement that helped education leaders achieve superintendent certification. Nancy proudly began her career as a teacher and principal in her home community of East San Jose, California, where she was the founding principal of Renaissance Academy, a California Distinguished School that was the highest-performing middle school in the district. She also led the successful effort to turn around the district's lowest-performing middle school. Nancy's work led to recognition by the Association of California School Administrators' Region 8 as the Middle School Principal of the Year, and she was honored by the University of California-Davis as a Rising Star. Nancy is a graduate of the inaugural cohort of the Harvard University Graduate School of Education's Doctor of Education Leadership (Ed.L.D.) program and a graduate of the Association of Latino Administrators and Superintendents Aspiring Superintendents Academy. She was also a Fall 2019 Pahara-Aspen Education Fellow, was named one of the top 100 most influential leaders in education in New York in 2020, and a San Jose State University Distinguished Alumna in 2023. She has served as an adjunct professor for New York University, Columbia University's Teachers College, and American University, as well as an expert guest at various Harvard Principals' Center Institutes. Nancy is a frequent keynote speaker and the coauthor of *Stay and Prevail: Students of Color Don't Need to Leave Their Communities to Succeed*. Nancy is a member of the board of directors at the Hunt Institute, Eye to Eye, Brightbeam, and serves as board chair for Education Leaders of Color (EdLoC).

▶ **Michelle Jarney** joined The Leadership Academy in 2004 and now serves as the Executive Director, Learning and Strategy. In that capacity, she helps lead internal capacity-building efforts, ensuring organizational sustainability and growth. As one of the designers of The Leadership Academy's signature coaching model, Michelle also coaches individual leaders and supports clients seeking to develop in-house expertise in leadership coaching. Additionally, she brings her extensive experience as a curriculum designer, facilitator, and consultant to a range of leadership development initiatives in districts throughout the country. Prior to her work with The Leadership Academy, Michelle was the Director of Education for the Union Square Partnership, where she developed an award-winning, public-private partnership that leveraged the resources of the private sector to support New York City public school students through innovative enrichment programs and career readiness opportunities. Michelle holds an M.A. and B.A. from Union College. Having reveled in games and puzzles as a child, Michelle continues to take great (perhaps excessive) pride in her ability to complete the *New York Times* Sunday crossword puzzle.

▶ **Michael Kim** joined The Leadership Academy in 2007 and now serves as the organization's Senior Director of Leadership Development and leads its national coaching services. As one of the designers of The Leadership Academy's signature coaching model, he trains the organization's coaches and external clients around developing in-house expertise in leadership coaching and implementing coaching programs. Michael also brings extensive experience as a curriculum designer and facilitator, project manager, and consultant to numerous districts and leadership development initiatives, including the New Leadership Relay for New York City, The Leadership Academy's New Principal Intensive, the West Michigan Leadership Academy, ACE Academy, Portland Public Schools (Oregon), Denver Public Schools (Colorado), and an i3/TISS grant from the US Department of Education. Prior to joining

The Leadership Academy, Michael served as an AmeriCorps member in Paterson, New Jersey, with the New Jersey Community Development Corporation and JFK High School's School-Based Youth Services Program. Michael holds a B.A. in psychology from Rutgers College and is a Certified Administrator of the Leadership Circle Profile™ 360° Assessment.

Introduction

> *Some people might say, "You don't need a coach anymore. You're such a good leader. Your school is doing very well…teacher capacity is already there. You have built trust within the community you serve. You're in a good place." But I have found that I needed that extra thought partner. With education consistently evolving, you need to have a partner you can trust, who you can confide in and share your next thinking with.*
>
> — New York City K–8 Principal

▶ ANISA'S STORY

Anisa stepped into the new middle school, the latest chapter in her educational career where she had recently been appointed principal, to be greeted by a scene of professional anticipation. Standing in the front office was a figure of considerable gravitas, waiting expressly for her. Although Anisa was no stranger to school leadership, this role marked her inaugural venture into spearheading a turnaround school, presenting unique challenges and opportunities for growth. The individual, clad in a suit that spoke of a seasoned career, extended a warm but urgent welcome to Anisa. He introduced himself as her *coach*. Over the next two hours, they engaged in a deep dive into his storied career as he shared his insights and detailed narratives of his experiences before retirement. Before leaving, he laid out a road map for Anisa, detailing strategic initiatives and critical actions for her to undertake during her initial weeks.

She barely got one word in.

Month after month, Anisa endured hours and hours of being talked at, each iteration compounded by growing levels of frustration, particularly when her coach's arrival necessitated abrupt departures from classrooms or pivotal parent meetings.

This form of "coaching" strayed far from an effective coaching experience and wasted Anisa's precious time as a principal. It was the opposite of what effective leadership coaching should entail.

Years later, Anisa found herself under the guidance of a new coach whose facilitative method was refreshingly collaborative and empowering. She and her coach would embark on insightful walkthroughs of classrooms. After each visit, the coach would engage Anisa with thoughtful prompts: "What did you observe? What questions does this raise for you? What feedback would you provide to that teacher?"

This shift in approach was transformational for Anisa. Her coach's questions pushed her outside her comfort zone, honing her instructional lens and challenging her to rethink what developing her teachers would require. It also changed Anisa's perspective on coaching. What was once a source of dread evolved into sessions she looked forward to with a mix of excitement and apprehension. Her coach helped her extend herself beyond what she was already confident in doing, and as she leaned into that learning edge, she grew as a leader.

This book is designed to guide you toward becoming a *Facilitative Competency-Based Coach*—one who encourages accountability in your coachees and creates a supportive and collaborative yet challenging environment that pushes them to their "learning edge," the place where true development and transformation occur.

▶ THE IMPACT OF COACHING

All educators have experienced a mixture of effective and ineffective professional learning. A 2020 survey told us that 98% of principals desire additional professional development, and an overwhelming number prefer support that is individualized and relevant to their specific needs and the needs of their schools (Levin et al., 2020).

When done well, leadership coaching can be a more effective form of professional development than traditional "sit and get" learning and can offer so many more benefits (Kissane-Long, 2012). Embedding leadership coaching into the school setting can deepen understanding of the school context and create the conditions for the coachee to learn on the job through the application of new skills that can be immediately applied; that is, leaders are able to reflect on and refine their leadership practices while they are enacting them (Huggins et al., 2021). Studies conducted in the last two decades have consistently found that coaches can play an important role in building the capacity of school leaders. Principals tell us that coaching improved their leadership skills and was the most valued of all their professional development opportunities (Darling-Hammond et al., 2022).

> We posit that one of the most effective forms of professional learning you could ever experience is coaching that utilizes a facilitative approach.

This kind of targeted support through leadership coaching keeps principals in their jobs longer – two times longer than the national average – and helps principals make real change in their schools (Drucker et al., 2018). With high-quality coaching, principals can attain higher teacher ratings, greater student achievement outcomes, and stronger instructional leadership practices (e.g., providing feedback to teachers, discussing actions and goals aligned with feedback) than those without coaches (Darling-Hammond et al., 2022). Yet only about half of principals nationwide were engaged in coaching as part of their professional development (Riley & Meredith, 2017). Our nation's students need more leaders with high-quality coaches.

Leadership coaching, when most effective, challenges leaders' thinking, provides effective and actionable feedback, and includes opportunities for reflection (Evans & Mohr, 1999). Darling-Hammond et al. (2022) found that the key features of high-quality coaching include:

- Skilled and well-prepared coaches.
- Coaches who hold a neutral position with the principal.
- Coaches who are provided with training and opportunities to work with colleagues in professional networks to support each other.

- An adequate number, length, and duration of coaching sessions to build skills, practice, reflect, and refine capacities in an iterative way.
- A system that supports leadership programs, including coaching and mentoring, and is involved in goal setting for those programs.

▶ THE LEADERSHIP ACADEMY'S COACHING JOURNEY

When we first created our flagship Aspiring Principals Program (APP) in New York City in 2003, we knew that once our graduates stepped into the principalship, they would need someone to support them in their new role. We identified experienced school leaders who would share tips and best practices, providing solid advice to guide principals through the labyrinth of ensuring compliance with innumerable rules and policies, navigating budgets, documenting performance, and organizing their time to get into classrooms.

But as any principal knows, leading a school is about so much more than those technical pieces. As new school leaders, many of our graduates struggled to move beyond putting out fires. They found they had limited bandwidth and capacity to do the critical work of identifying their school's challenges and working with their teams to find and dig up the roots of those challenges to make sustainable change. We realized they needed a thought partner, someone who could create space for them to take a step back, reflect on their work, and consider how they needed to shift the way they thought about or acted on the intractable challenges in their schools (Nadurak, 2018).

We needed coaches who empowered leaders to solve their own problems and fostered the deep leadership growth necessary to change outcomes for students. Drawing from years of research on a wide range of effective leadership and coaching models, concepts, frameworks, and tools, we created a unique *Facilitative Competency-Based (FCB) Coaching* approach. These essential beliefs about adult learning form the conceptual underpinnings of our coaching methodology.

- We believe that adults learn most deeply from experience and reflection.
- We believe learning is a social process.
- We believe unlearning is inherent in transformative learning.
- We believe adults rely on stories to make meaning.
- We believe adults learn best in an environment of structured freedom.

Ababio-Fernandez and Winkfield (2023) remind us,

> What stands true…is the need for leaders to have the technical, emotional, situational, strategic, and instructional knowledge of managing schools and districts while simultaneously moving the organization and its people toward the urgent cause of success.
>
> (p. 32)

FCB Coaching aims to build these types of leaders.

▶ THE NORTH STAR REMAINS INCLUSIVE, MEANINGFUL, AND RIGOROUS CLASSROOM ENVIRONMENTS

As The Leadership Academy's definition of "equity" states, this work is about every school and school system being intentionally built to ensure children of every race, ethnicity, language or other characteristics achieve academic, social, and emotional success. We see coaching as an essential tool for achieving equity because becoming more equitable takes constant work both on ourselves and on our environment. This "self-work" is at the core of coaching. Importantly, this coaching, while focused on shifting adult behavior, must always be in service of rigorous, meaningful and deeply engaging instructional environments that affirm identity and create inclusive spaces for all students. Coaches are not changing behaviors merely to improve individuals; rather, their emphasis is on supporting adults to modify their decision-making and actions to better serve the needs of students.

We believe this coaching practice creates the space for consistent, high-leverage feedback that will help educators move closer to creating culturally responsive classrooms, schools and school systems. Considerations include how leaders ensure that all students have access to high-quality teaching and learning, create conditions for students to help shape the learning environment, and elevate high-quality instructional materials that provide students "windows" and "mirrors" of different experiences.

Throughout this book, you will find resources and tools to apply an FCB Coaching approach across all levels within a school system. This coherent approach to adult learning and change within a system is necessary to ensure all adults are equipped with the skills and mindsets to shift learning experiences, and thus outcomes, for all students.

▶ LOOKING AHEAD

Each chapter in this book will provide you with foundational concepts and a series of tools, frameworks, strategies, or techniques to build your FCB Coaching skills. Interspersed throughout each chapter, you will find case studies. Although the names of the principals and coaches in these case studies are fictitious, the stories describe real-life situations that highlight specific concepts and practices. At the end of each chapter, you will find a set of "Back to You" questions and immediate actions you can undertake to help you closely examine and improve your own coaching practice – FCB Coaching involves self-reflection, learning, and growth of both the coach and coachee. Finally, in the appendices, you will find additional tools to incorporate into your coaching moving forward.

In **Chapter 1**, we will explore the underpinnings of FCB Coaching, define what it looks like in practice and dig into the discrete skills, behaviors, and actions that comprise what FCB Coaches need to know and be able to do. FCB Coaching is a job-embedded iterative approach to school and system leadership development in which two people (the coach and coachee) work together around an agreed-upon set of skills, knowledge and behaviors (competencies). FCB Coaches target and customize coaching to develop their coachee's capacity to improve teaching and learning, dismantle systemic inequities, and transform their organizations.

In **Chapter 2**, we will explore The Leadership Academy's six *Equity Leadership Dispositions*, which form the foundation for FCB Coaching. The Leadership Academy believes that leadership isn't effective unless the leader is culturally responsive – recognizing the impact of institutionalized racism on their own lives and the lives of the students and families they work with and actively and intentionally working to mitigate, disrupt, and dismantle systemic oppression. A leadership coach must understand how to coach with a lens that develops the *self* in service of the *system* and cultivates the academic success of all students. This chapter unpacks the six *Equity Leadership Dispositions*, and in doing so, it helps coaches explore how to improve their own cultural competence and design sessions to develop culturally responsive leaders.

Chapter 3 provides guidance on how to initiate a new coaching relationship. The five steps in this chapter will help foster a shared understanding of the purpose of the coaching relationship and create a set of agreements that will maximize learning and development. Coaches will learn what basic logistics for clear and effective communication channels need to be agreed upon. This chapter also includes a set of suggested practices to use when setting mutual goals necessary to achieve success. Finally, it provides tips to address any potential disengagement early in the coaching relationship.

Chapter 4 focuses on creating the conditions to build trust and help coachees achieve meaningful self-awareness and leadership growth to become culturally responsive leaders. Trust is built *through* coaching by providing care, exhibiting competence, being reliable, and expressing sincerity. With trust, the coach can gain a deeper understanding of how their coachee perceives and makes meaning of their world, which in turn strengthens the relationship and enables the coach to tailor sessions to provide deeper and more impactful learning. This chapter describes how coaches can acknowledge and challenge mental models, help their coachees climb down the Ladder of Inference, and use questions effectively.

Chapter 5 introduces several concepts and techniques to help engage in the challenging conversations that are necessary to bring the coachee to the learning edge, enabling them to achieve meaningful, systemic improvements in pursuit of the north star – academic, social, and emotional success for all students. Since discomfort is often an inherent part of learning, this chapter discusses the importance of creating a "holding environment," a safe learning space for coachees to attain greater levels of personal insight as they grow in their capacity to be culturally responsive leaders. We provide strategies for how to provide a balance of support and challenge to keep leaders in a "productive zone of disequilibrium." The chapter offers ways to provide meaningful feedback and use deeper levels of dialogue to address adaptive challenges. The chapter also describes how to help coachees use systems thinking to uncover the root causes of organizational challenges and catalyze meaningful change.

Chapter 6 takes a deep dive into the full arc of the coaching relationship and offers practical ways the coach can plan coaching sessions to maximize impact. Seeing the bigger picture of the coaching engagement from beginning to end and zooming in for individual coaching sessions supports the coach in strategically planning for greater success and impact. This chapter provides a (CPR)^2 structure that can be used to plan each individual coaching session, and it shares ideas and resources that can be used during coaching sessions.

At The Leadership Academy, we know the greatest asset in all organizations is its people. That is why we believe coaching is an intrinsic aspect of leadership and the responsibility of all leaders. Although the charge principals and district leaders are given often relates to overall school and systems improvement, the core of their work is about capacity building – of all staff members. No matter your title, if you are a coach or take a coaching stance with the people you work with in schools or school systems, this book is for you.

Bibliography

Ababio-Fernandez, R., & Winkfield, C. (2023). *Shifting self and system: How educational leaders propel excellent for achieving equity.* Corwin.

Aguas, M. J. (2019). Millennial and generation Z's perspectives on leadership effectiveness. *Emerging Leadership Journeys, 1*(13). https://www.regent.edu/journal/emerging-leadership-journeys/gen-z-generation-z-leadership/

Breibur, S. (June 25, 2018). *Supporting novice teachers: Tips for z-friendly professional development.* ACSD. https://www.ascd.org/blogs/supporting-novice-teachers-tips-for-z-friendly-professional-development

Darling-Hammond, L., Wechsler, M. E., Levin, S., Leung-Gagné, M., & Tozer, S. (2022). *Developing effective principals: What kind of learning matters?* [Report]. Learning Policy Institute.

Demirbilek, M., & Keser, S. (2022). Leadership expectations of Generation Z teachers working in educational organizations. *Research in Educational Administration & Leadership, 7*(1), 209–245.

Drucker, K., Grossman, J., & Nagler, N. (2018). *Still in the game: How coaching keeps leaders in schools and making progress.* The New York City Leadership Academy.

Evans, P. M., & Mohr, N. (1999). Professional development for principals: Seven core beliefs. *Phi Delta Kappa International, 80*(7), 530–532.

Huggins, K. S., Klar, H. W., & Andreoli, P. M. (2021). Facilitating leadership coach capacity for school leadership development: The intersection of structured community and experiential learning. *Educational Administration Quarterly, 57*(1), 82–112.

Kissane-Long, A. L. (2012). *Using mentor-coaching to refine instructional supervision skills of developing principals* [Doctoral dissertation]. Los Angeles: University of California. https://eric.ed.gov/?id=ED547469

Levin, S., Leung, M., Edgerton, A. K., & Scott, C. (2020). *Elementary school principals' professional learning: Current status and future needs.* Learning Policy Institute.

Lewis, L., & Scott, J. (2020). *Principal professional development in U.S. Public Schools in 2017–18.* Stats in Brief NCES 2020-045. U.S. Department of Education. Institute of Education Sciences, National Center for Education Statistics.

Nadurak, K. (July 23, 2018). Learning how to develop lead learners: Lessons from our first 15 years. *Leadership Insights*. The Leadership Academy.

Riley, D. L., & Meredith, J. (2017). *State efforts to strengthen school leadership: Insights from CCSSO actions groups*. Policy Studies Associates. https://wallacefoundation.org/report/state-efforts-strengthen-school-leadership-insights-ccsso-action-groups-insights-ccsso

Sparks, S. (2023). *Keeping principals on the job: These numbers show how*. EdWeek. https://www.edweek.org/leadership/keeping-principals-on-the-job-these-numbers-show-how/2023/08

Style, E. (1996). Curriculum as window and mirror. *Social Science Record, 33*(2), 19–23. https://www.nationalseedproject.org/Key-SEED-Texts/curriculum-as-window-and-mirror

Will, M. (January 16, 2020). *Here's what Gen Z teachers around the world want in their jobs*. EdWeek. https://www.edweek.org/teaching-learning/heres-what-gen-z-teachers-around-the-world-want-in-their-jobs/2020/01

Unpacking Facilitative Competency-Based Coaching

"We're not coaching someone to be compliant with the district mandates. We are coaching someone to grow their skillset to better serve children and families."

– Leadership Academy Coach

> **BIG IDEAS IN THIS CHAPTER**
>
> - Coaching is about transforming individuals in the service of transforming systems. The goal is to create rigorous, meaningful, and deeply engaging instructional environments that affirm identity and create inclusive spaces for all students.
> - *Facilitative Competency-Based (FCB) Coaching* is a job-embedded iterative approach to school and system leadership development in which two people (coach and coachee) work together around an agreed-upon and customized set of skills, knowledge and behaviors (competencies).

Good coaches help leaders develop the *self* in *service* of the *system*. Indeed, effective coaching is bigger than serving one individual leader's learning needs. Coaching conversations can be used as a primary lever to shift instructional practice, address inequities, and bring about organizational change. Systemic inequities and racism are deeply embedded in the long-standing policies and practices of so many schools and school systems. Identifying and dismantling them requires vision and a deep understanding of bias and how it pervades our education systems. It requires strong leadership.

▶ FCB COACHING

Facilitative Competency-Based Coaching is a job-embedded and iterative process in which two people (coach and coachee) work together around an agreed-upon set of skills, knowledge and behaviors (competencies). Through this tailored approach, the goal is to not only identify areas for improvement but to actively facilitate the development journey, expanding the coachee's capacity to become a more effective leader.

FCB Coaches:

- Proficiently use questions and provide feedback that is ongoing and authentic, and honors coachees' unique needs. The feedback and questions serve to develop coachees' instructional leadership capacity to critically reflect on their practice and shift their behaviors, thinking, and mindsets to make systemic changes in their schools, school systems, and classrooms.
- Are critical thought partners who can create a confidential and safe space for the educator to reflect without fear of judgment or evaluation. The coach must provide a balance of supportive and challenging experiences to enable the coachee to critically examine their own thinking, behaviors, biases, and actions to reach their learning edge.
- Build the capacity of coachees to proactively identify and dismantle inequities and create inclusive systems that meet the needs of the students. Doing so requires adaptive change; it requires leaders and their teams to reflect on their own biases and then change behaviors and beliefs. Just-in-time problem-solving and strategizing will always be a part of coaching, but the greater goal is to support leaders in developing the skills, knowledge, and dispositions necessary for equity-focused, culturally responsive leadership.
- Tailor their coaching to the needs of the leader, their students, their team, and the system they lead. Unlike many

other coaching models, FCB Coaching is not a one-size-fits-all, prescriptive model. It creates a deeper level of self-awareness that allows the leader to thrive in multiple settings and contexts. In our more than 20 years of education leadership coaching, we have found that this kind of targeted support enables leaders to stay in their jobs longer and make real, sustainable change.

With FCB Coaching, the coach creates an environment in which the education leader engages in critical and targeted reflection on their practice with the goal of *facilitating* the paradigm or behavioral shifts necessary to become a culturally responsive leader. A culturally responsive leader recognizes the impact of institutionalized racism on their own lives and the lives of the students and families they work with and actively and intentionally works to mitigate, disrupt, and dismantle systemic oppression. The Leadership Academy's six *Equity Leadership Dispositions*, which will be explored further in Chapter 2, represent the mindsets and behaviors that our experience and research has found enable leaders to eradicate inequities and truly transform their schools and systems in the service of all students.

As depicted in our theory of action (Figure 1.1), the ultimate beneficiary of FCB Coaching is the **student**; the coach's moves

Figure 1.1 FCB Coaching Theory of Action

©The Leadership Academy

should aim to help coachees shift their mindset and behaviors so they can improve instructional practice and better serve the needs of their students and schools. As such, FCB Coaches make direct links to the ultimate outcomes and purpose of the schooling process: to ensure students are academically, emotionally, and socially prepared to lead fulfilling, choice-filled lives and contribute meaningfully to a diverse world. Taking an FCB approach in the classroom involves shifting *from*:

- Formal authority-based conversations *to* coaching conversations.
- Rhetoric-based rubric feedback *to* feedback grounded in low inference that explicitly calls out the impact of behaviors and actions.
- Focus-less classroom observations *to* observations with a teacher-informed specific focus driven by school instructional priorities and student needs.
- Scheduled classroom observations *to* a culture of frequent observations and shared ownership tailored to the learning needs of instructional staff.
- Feedback offered through email, evaluations and sticky notes *to* the expectation that every piece of feedback requires a coaching conversation to listen, question, and reflect.
- Random acts of professional learning and coaching *to* purposeful professional learning and intentional coaching undergirded by research-based beliefs in how adults learn best.

▶ WHAT SHOULD AN FCB COACH KNOW AND BE ABLE TO DO?

The following boxes describe in detail the expected actions of an effective FCB Coach. We've broken these up into three thematic areas: Who are we and why are we together; where do we want to go, and how will we get there? These themes are interconnected, and the practice of coaching is an iterative one. Throughout this book, we will introduce concepts, tools, and ideas that you can use to build the skills, knowledge, and abilities that you will need to successfully undertake the actions outlined here.

Theme 1: Build Relationships and Learn Context

Relationships are key for coaching to be successful. The coach needs to understand what they contribute to the relationship, who the education leader is and where they come from, and what the education leader is experiencing. A central question for this theme of coaching is, "Who are we as coaches and education leaders, and why are we together?"

THEME 1 Who Are We and Why Are We Together?
Build Relationships and Learn Context

Set parameters for an effective coaching relationship by:	Developing a shared understanding of what makes for an effective coaching relationship and establishing norms and expectations to that end. Characteristics of an effective coaching relationship include mutual trust, vulnerability, honesty, respect, follow-through, feedback, an openness to learning, and prioritizing time together.
	Articulating what coaching is and isn't, distinguishing it from counseling, therapy, and other forms of leadership development, and situating it within a framework for meaningful adult learning.
	Naming leadership needs that will and will not be addressed through coaching and helping the leader determine how to meet learning needs that are outside the purview of coaching.
	Defining and ensuring terms of confidentiality with the education leader and their organization, as applicable.

(Continued)

THEME 1 (Continued)

Establish a foundation for equity and culturally responsive practice by:	Coming to a shared understanding of what coach and coachee mean by "equity." For example, at The Leadership Academy, equity means that every school and school system is intentionally built to ensure children of every race, ethnicity, language, or other characteristics of their identities have what they need to achieve academic, social, and emotional success.
	Understanding what culturally responsive practice is and elevating it as a frame for the work. A culturally responsive leader recognizes the impact of institutionalized racism on their own lives and the lives of the students and families they work with, and actively and intentionally works to mitigate, disrupt, and dismantle systemic oppression.
Nurture an authentic relationship with the education leader by:	Recognizing the intersections of one's own identity markers, experiences of privilege and/or oppression, and triggers and biases; understanding how those things have affected one's journey and perspectives and using professional judgment in sharing those aspects of self; creating the space for the coachee to do the same.
	Establishing and maintaining a mutual stance of trust, honesty, confidentiality, and learning; demonstrating curiosity and care for the education leader, accepting them as a whole and capable person with intersectional identities, strengths and weaknesses, hopes and fears, and the same basic needs that all people share.

(Continued)

THEME 1 (Continued)

Learn about the education leader as a person and leader by:	Eliciting and observing in action the education leader's beliefs, values, intersectional identities, mental models, hopes and fears, strengths and challenges, and overall vision for their organization (school, district, etc.); searching for confirming and disconfirming evidence and connections and disconnects between what is stated and enacted.
	Uncovering how the education leader sets priorities and makes meaning of their leadership role; noticing the leader's feelings, assumptions, and beliefs about equity and related behaviors.
	Getting behind the "eyes" of the education leader by learning what they pay attention to, what motivates them, what they are afraid of, and what is important to them.
Learn about the education leader as a learner by:	Identifying how the education leader learns and makes meaning of the current state and historical context of the organization and the evidence for the conclusions they are drawing.
	Noticing what data has been selected, gathered, and analyzed, and the way that information is narrated and interpreted by the education leader and exploring what additional data and conversations are needed to develop a more complete picture of the leader.
	Recognizing patterns and trends about the default learning style of the education leader; determining approaches that effectively create the conditions for the education leader to grapple or reckon with a presenting issue.

(Continued)

THEME 1 (Continued)

Learning about the education leader's context by:	Gathering data from multiple sources (formal, anecdotal, and observational) to understand organizational performance and context from different perspectives. This could include learning more about/from key players: system mandates; community needs, history, and relationship with the education leader's organization; school climate; attendance; student performance; and family involvement; use the data to identify patterns and trends, systems, processes, and structures, and mental models that underlie the current state of the organization.
	Using data to assess the state of equity in the organization and its community, such as data related to resource allocation and utilization, hiring and staff composition, student services, and linguistic and cultural supports.

Theme 2: Establishing Coaching Purpose and Goal Setting

In learning about a leader and their context, the coach is actively exploring how to support the coachee's leadership development. Coaching encompasses far more than just trusting relationships and supportive conversations. It is designed to raise leaders' conscious awareness of how and what they can improve and to facilitate the development of leadership skills, ways of being, and habits of mind necessary to lead for equity and excellence on behalf of students. Determining where to focus those efforts is a collaborative process and requires thoughtful decision-making and continuous learning on the part of both coach and coachee, about the leader, the organization and its learners, and the greater context in which they find themselves. The work of coaching is always aligned to purpose and core values. A central question for this theme is, "Where do we need to go?"

THEME 2 Where Do We Need to Go?
Establishing Coaching Purpose and Goal Setting

Explore and identify organizational goals by:	Eliciting the education leader's understanding of organizational dynamics and determining the implications for organizational goal setting; engaging the leader in continuously identifying and using multiple measures of data to assess the current state of the organization, formulate hypotheses about organizational needs and points of leverage, set priorities for focus and action, and adjust over time. In doing so, specifically analyze and make transparent data related to equity.
	Challenging the leader to set ambitious but attainable improvement goals for key areas of the organization. This includes discussing and identifying with the educational leader the systems, processes, and practices that do not serve the needs of all students effectively or that contribute to inequity in the organization and its broader context.
Determine leadership competencies to strengthen and prioritize development by:	Considering the *Equity Leadership Dispositions* and actions involved in creating culturally responsive learning environments in which all students can thrive; introducing and using multiple tools with the leader (including direct questioning and self-evaluations, 360s, and feedback from others) to support them in assessing their learning edges.
	Gathering confirming and disconfirming evidence from multiple sources to gain a more specific, nuanced, and in-depth understanding of the coachee's leadership. This can include observing the education leader in multiple contexts and having conversations with the leader to explore their feelings, ideas, perceptions, behaviors, mental models, and concerns.
	Supporting the leader in making explicit and transparent the leadership growth they are striving for and the rationale for doing so; Asking open-ended questions that create greater clarity, possibility, or insight; providing feedback and guiding the leader in continually testing, adjusting, refining, changing, and communicating as needed.

(Continued)

THEME 2 (Continued)

Support the education leader in envisioning and determining pathways to change by:	Supporting the leader in articulating a robust vision for success built on the actions and practices of culturally responsive schools and school systems.
	Guiding the leader in assessing capacity and unpacking the personal, interpersonal, and systemic shifts required to achieve that vision; supporting the leader in building coherent understanding of the multiple levels of work in the overall improvement system, including the interplay between the leader's priorities for growth, the needs of the organization and its learners, and the many external goals and demands placed upon them.
	Engaging the leader in exploring the actions needed to facilitate change and in creating opportunities to experiment with new practices to support the desired shifts; throughout the process, supporting the leader in considering and anticipating intended and unintended consequences of priorities and proposed actions.
Develop and reflect on one's development and approach as a coach by:	Conceptualizing what coaching the education leader entails, considering what has been learned about the coachee as a person, leader, and learner; identifying the coaching practices and strategies needed to develop and fortify the coachee's leadership capacity.
	Tailoring the coaching engagement to maximize the coachee's learning and making decisions regarding optimal pacing and sequencing; purposefully and strategically utilizing a combination of facilitative and directive approaches, being mindful of how the two work together.
	Creating space for reflection on one's own mental models related to identity and equity; actively exploring assumptions and biases and considering how one's own coaching practices impede or support the education leader's development.
	Establishing one's own goals for coaching development, including knowledge and skill building, in order to improve practice.

Theme 3: Fostering Learning and Achieving Results

Learning for the coach, the education leader, and the organization are interwoven and ongoing during coaching. The ultimate goal of coaching is to foster effective leadership to improve outcomes for ALL students. The education leader, their organization, and the coach must all do their part to achieve the desired results. A key role of the coach is supporting the leader in becoming increasingly independent in their learning and leadership development, helping them to explore the difficult aspects of learning that they must engage with to make change. The competencies in this section build on the coaching purpose and coaching relationship described in the previous themes. First we discussed, "Who are we and why are we together?" Then we explored, "Where do we need to go?" This final theme asks, "How will we get there?"

THEME 3 How Will We Get There?
Fostering Learning and Achieving Results

Create a holding environment of support and challenge by:	Drawing out and leveraging the education leader's strengths; acknowledging the leader's successes and learning.
	Accepting that there will be discomfort for both the coach and the education leader in the inquiry, reflection, and feedback process as one creates cognitive dissonance. Provoke and contain that discomfort to maximize learning, balancing challenge and support so the leader can explore change and sustain the energy that the exploration requires.
	Articulating in advance the cognitive dissonance they will experience so when they encounter it, they recognize it as an opportunity for growth.

(Continued)

THEME 3 (Continued)

Listen deeply and ask questions to understand and support the education leader by:	Focusing completely on the leader and observing body language, choice of words, inflection, and what is said and not said. Use silence and wait time. Clarify, summarize, paraphrase, and use other strategies to deepen understanding.
	Noticing what one is listening to and for as a coach and the quality of the listening and thinking environment created; listening to fortify the relationship; to understand the leader's ways of being, thinking, seeing, feeling, and acting; and to support the leader in processing their emotions and understanding their own meaning making.
	Using different question types to promote extended dialogue and evoke discovery and insight; supporting the leader in recognizing their mental models and biases; provoking cognitive dissonance for the leader to examine the discrepancies between thoughts/actions and perception/actuality and identify limiting assumptions and fixed mindsets.
	Engaging in authentic inquiry to explore and identify the matters before the leader, learning more about them, considering outcomes, and encouraging commitment to action.
Share effective feedback by:	Considering how aspects of identity and power are at play in the selection, delivery, and impact of the feedback; framing feedback to optimize impact, considering the leader's context, learning preferences, and timing to ensure benefit.
	Providing feedback that is timely, applicable, useful, honest, purposeful, and based on low inference data and observation; being cognizant of emotional tenor, eye contact, body language, and impact.

(Continued)

THEME 3 (Continued)

Embody the stance of a coach by:	Being open and willing to manage multiple and simultaneous tensions that are inherent to coaching. This includes maintaining credibility while being a public learner who engages in authentic inquiry, balancing humility with competence, being fully present in the moment while staying focused on a bigger picture, concentrating on the education leader and the context while being attuned to one's self (including one's own biases, limitations, goals, and learning), and giving one's full self to the coaching relationship while maintaining objectivity about the leader's goals, problems, and context.
	Modeling transparency and metacognition in one's coaching, sharing what one is doing, why one is doing it, and what one does and does not know; being aware of one's emotional state and the implications for coaching; eliciting feedback about what is effective and not effective in one's coaching.
	Reflecting on one's coaching and one's learning about coaching, recognizing sticking points and exploring new possibilities to move past them.
Facilitate self-directed learning in service of coaching goals by:	Developing and using a diverse set of coaching strategies and tools that allow the leader to increase their understanding of self, implicate themselves in the situation and system they are in, take ownership of their learning, and champion equity.
	Identifying opportunities for the leader (within coaching sessions and outside of them) to experiment with new ideas and actions, explore and evaluate possibilities, demonstrate and practice leadership skills, and create and deepen new learning.
	Instilling the habits of reflection and adaptive leadership in the leader. Guiding their reflection on self, leadership, change, and the organization, helping them to step outside the moment. Over time, adopting a less active guiding role as reflection becomes increasingly self-directed by the leader.

(Continued)

THEME 3 (Continued)

Cultivate and sustain accountability by:	Engaging the leader in leading cycles of improvement, maintaining energy and focus on the organization's aspirational goals, benchmarking progress toward those goals regularly, and adjusting actions as necessary in service of creating the conditions for all students to be successful.
	Ensuring a dynamic holding environment, grounding feedback, and opportunities for reflection in the actions and dispositions of culturally responsive leaders; eliciting commitment to action from the leader, checking for follow-through on stated actions, supporting the leader in assessing the impact of those actions, and connecting coaching sessions across time.
	Positioning the leader to independently construct new knowledge, sustain learning, and continue advancing equity after the coaching engagement ends.

▶ INCORPORATING AN FCB COACHING APPROACH: JORDYN'S STORY

Jordyn, once a superintendent and principal, dedicated her life to nurturing future leaders. Her coaching was anchored in the warm relationships she established with her coachees, and she regularly provided resources, insights, and helpful suggestions based on her considerable experience and expertise. She also gave her coachees feedback, finding ways to sprinkle it in. "I would make a bad news sandwich," she told us. I'd say something positive, then slip in the feedback, and then I'd make sure to say something else positive, so when my coachees left, they always felt good.

Jordyn knew that in most engagements, she was able to help leaders solve the problems they were encountering in the moment. However, she was increasingly aware that her coachees' schools were remaining stagnant with persistent patterns of disproportionality and low achievement. When she talked about this with her principals, they attributed the lack of progress to all sorts of factors – the central office, inexperienced staff, and even the students and their families – but they rarely implicated themselves.

After participating in an FCB Coaching training session, Jordyn began to question the very foundation of her coaching philosophy. While rapport with coachees remained crucial, Jordyn wanted to challenge her principals to own their role in making the changes that would lead to different outcomes for their students. She knew that would mean pushing her coachees to their learning edges, something that would likely create at least some discomfort for them and for her!

This evolution in her coaching approach was not easy. Jordyn spent time practicing and refining her listening, questioning, and feedback skills, realizing coaching was not just about asking questions – but about asking the right questions. She had her coachees reflect on their beliefs and reckon with their biases. She asked them to articulate what they wanted instruction to look like and examined with them how that compared to what they saw in their classrooms. She asked them to envision the implications for professional learning and how they saw their role in building the capacity of their staff. She also gave them plenty of direct feedback so they could see the impact of their own actions and adjust accordingly. Whether they were walking the building, debriefing a meeting, or looking at data, Jordyn made sure her coachees were the ones doing the heavy lifting as they considered the mindset and behavioral shifts critical to achieving their goals.

Jordyn shifted her coaching practices in several key ways. She focused on building her coachees' capacity to make the changes that would result in different experiences and outcomes for their students, and she found ways to engage her coachees in ways that pushed their thinking and held them accountable as they considered new paths forward. In the next chapter, we will dig deeper into the dispositions we seek to develop in leaders, and then in the rest of this book, we will help you transform your coaching practice just as Jordyn did.

▶ FINAL THOUGHTS

A great coach is committed to their work with education leaders not merely for an individual leader's sake but on behalf of all students. They target and customize coaching based on student, school, and school system needs and develop the leader's capacity to improve teaching and learning, address inequity, and facilitate organizational change. The work of a coach is not only about professional learning for the coachee. Becoming an effective facilitative coach requires self-reflection and learning for the coach as well.

BACK TO YOU

- To what extent does your coaching reflect the FCB Coaching approach? *Think back on your last coaching session and assess how much of your coaching practice exhibits this approach versus a more traditional style.*
- In what ways does your coaching already demonstrate what an FCB Coach should know and be able to do? *Identify a theme or particular action to continue refining or further developing in your practice.*
- How do you make sure that individual development efforts contribute effectively to overall systems improvement and more equitable student and classroom practices? *Write down a success story or a personal goal.*

Bibliography

Aguilar, E. (2013). *The art of coaching: Effective strategies for school transformation* [Kindle version]. Jossey-Bass.

Aguilar, E. (2020). *Coaching for equity: Conversations that change practice* [Kindle version]. Jossey-Bass.

Bloom, G. (2005). *Blended coaching: Skills and strategies to support principal development.* Corwin Press.

Bloom, G., & Wilson, J. (2023). *Blended coaching.* Sage Publications, Inc.

Colorado Department of Education. (2010). *Equity toolkit for administrators.* https://www.cde.state.co.us/postsecondary/equitytoolkit

Dweck, C. (2006). *Mindset: The new psychology of success* [Kindle version]. Ballantine Books.

Grissom, J. A., Egalite, A. J., & Lindsay, C. A. (2021). *How principals affect students and schools: A systematic synthesis of two decades of research.* The Wallace Foundation. https://wallacefoundation.org/report/how-principals-affect-students-and-schools-systematic-synthesis-two-decades-research

Heifetz, R. (1994). *Leadership without easy answers.* Harvard University Press.

Helms, J. (1990). *Black and white racial identity: Theory, research and practice.* Greenwood Press.

Kegan, R. (1994). *In over our heads: The mental demands of modern life.* Harvard University Press.

National Center for Cultural Competence. (2016). *Definitions of cultural competence.* http://www.nccccurricula.info/culturalcompetence.html

Quigley, D. (2016). *Building cultural competence in environmental studies and natural resource sciences. Society & Natural Resources,* 29(6), 725–737.

Tatum, B. D. (1992). *Talking about race, learning about racism: The application of racial identity development theory in the classroom. Harvard Educational Review,* 62(1), 1–24.

Yasharian, F. (2016). Improving on Strength: Developing coaching competencies for the NYC leadership academy [Doctoral dissertation]. Harvard Graduate School of Education. https://dash.harvard.edu/handle/1/27013347

Chapter 2

Centering Equity in Leadership Coaching

> "Coaching helped me envision how I wanted to show up as a leader."
> – Former High School Principal

BIG IDEAS IN THIS CHAPTER

- Leadership is not effective unless it is culturally responsive. The Leadership Academy's six *Equity Leadership Dispositions* describe the foundational aspects of what it takes to be a culturally responsive leader.
- A culturally responsive leader develops the *self* in service of creating a *system* that cultivates the academic, social, and emotional success of all students.
- *Facilitative Competency-Based (FCB) Coaching* builds leaders' capacity within the *Equity Leadership Dispositions* to ensure that the learning environment they foster is designed to meet the needs of every single student.

A culturally responsive leader recognizes the impact of institutionalized racism on their own lives and the lives of the students and families they work with and actively and intentionally works to mitigate, disrupt, and dismantle systemic oppression. For leaders to develop and sustain the skills they need to lead schools in this way, they need to continuously reflect and shift the way they think and act.

▶ IMAGINE...

Imagine walking into a classroom where students' identities are affirmed and reflected in the curriculum, where students are held to high expectations and given the support needed to access grade-level, rigorous content. Imagine the tasks students are given not only assess students' knowledge of standards but invite them to critique and challenge systems around them as agents of change.

Imagine speaking with families and community members who feel like true partners to teachers and staff members, and who experience the school and school system as responsive to their needs. Imagine a classroom in which the diverse perspectives and voices of those families are celebrated and empowered so that their children can meet their full potential.

Imagine meeting the principal, who embodies the culturally responsive leadership dispositions necessary to shift adult practice and mindsets across the school, who coaches teachers and staff members to build inclusive and rigorous classroom and community spaces, and who cultivates a community of care and authentic engagement with families.

Now, finally, imagine walking into a central office that supports culturally responsive principals across their system – prioritizing the capacity building and investment in the adults who dedicate themselves to serving students and families. Imagine resources that are coordinated to develop schools in ways that meet their unique needs and tackle problems of practice identified by the school community. Imagine a central office that takes a comprehensive and strategic approach to cultivating the types of schools its leaders want for their own children and loved ones. Imagine a central office that centers and elevates family and community partnerships as a key part of their vision and mission.

This is what an effective culturally responsive leader builds.

Creating a learning environment where every student thrives does not just magically happen. It requires a particular kind of leadership. School leaders are central to student success. In fact, research has found that school leaders have as great an impact on student learning as teachers do (Grissom et al., 2021). Their data from more than 22,000 principals showed us that an above-average principal, on average, provides three months more learning in reading and math for a student in that school over the year compared to a below-average principal. Schools with more effective principals have lower absentee rates, high teacher job satisfaction, and reduced turnover of effective teachers (Grissom et al., 2021). Effective principals focus on instruction, create a productive school climate, facilitate collaboration and professional learning communities, and make strategic personnel and resource management decisions.

Being culturally responsive is not an add-on but essential and necessary given our diversifying demographics and the intersectional identities we serve. At The Leadership Academy, our mission is to build the capacity of educational leaders, at every level of the system, to confront inequities and create the conditions necessary for all students to thrive.

▶ SIX EQUITY LEADERSHIP DISPOSITIONS

The Leadership Academy's six *Equity Leadership Dispositions* (Figure 2.1) represent the mindsets and behaviors that our experience and research have found enable leaders to dismantle inequities and transform their schools. FCB Coaches help their coachees become culturally responsive leaders by building their ability to exhibit the behaviors described in each of the following dispositions. After each disposition, we offer some coaching questions to explore with your coachee.

REFLECT: Reflect on Personal Assumptions, Beliefs, and Behaviors

Personal beliefs determine how an individual sees the world, other people, and oneself (Nelson & Guerra, 2014). Our beliefs and unconscious biases determine our actions and practices,

Centering Equity in Leadership Coaching 31

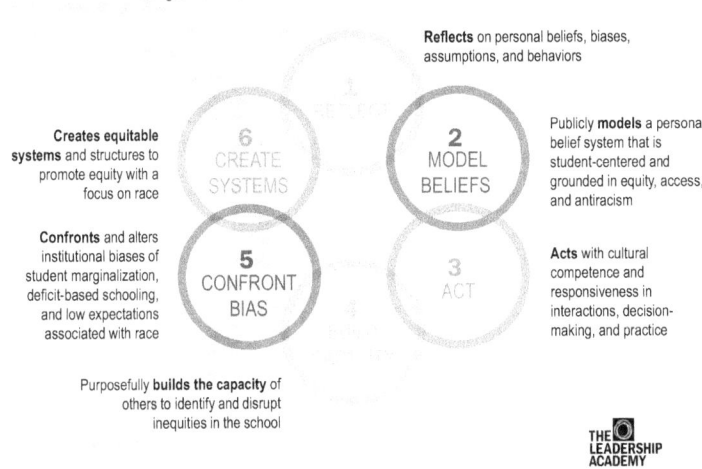

Figure 2.1 The Leadership Academy's Six *Equity Leadership Dispositions*

©The Leadership Academy

and these actions inform how systems develop and operate, including our current education system (Berg, 2018). For leaders to feel comfortable addressing issues of bias, inequity, and race, they first need to have a heightened understanding of their own identities, values, assumptions, and biases (Brown, 2004; Gooden & O'Doherty, 2015). In addition to this self-exploration, leaders must cultivate and maintain a deep understanding of how privilege, power, and oppression operate historically and currently in school and society (Galloway & Ishimaru, 2017). Without a firm self-examination of their own identity and role in historically inequitable structures, leaders risk reproducing inequities inside and outside their schools and systems (Brooks et al., 2007; Jones & Vagule, 2013; Rigby & Tredway, 2015). As leaders of diverse communities, such critical self-reflection should be an ongoing, lifelong process (Brown, 2004).

Culturally responsive leaders live this disposition by:

- Recognizing the privileges and unearned advantages they might hold based on position, identity, or background.

- Committing to lifelong personal examination of how their biases and lived experiences impact their lens.
- Continuously examining and reflecting on how their role in the system might contribute to or support inequitable practices.
- Actively seeking to learn how privilege, power, and oppression operate historically and currently within their context.
- Seeking feedback and looking for low-inference evidence to help reflect on where and how they are being responsive and where and how they are missing the mark.

Possible coaching questions:

- How do the intersections of your identity impact your leadership?
- What is your personal vision and belief system around diversity, equity, inclusion, and belonging?
- In what ways do your experiences align with or diverge from those of the students you serve?

MODEL BELIEFS: Publicly Model a Personal Belief System That Is Grounded in Equity

Culturally responsive leaders must demonstrate that addressing inequities is a priority. Leaders accomplish this by consistently naming equity as a driving force behind leadership actions and decisions. By taking a strong and vocal stance, leaders communicate the value of equity across all practices and can establish a coherent and common purpose for members of the learning community (Rigby & Tredway, 2015). To help others build their skill and will to examine the impact of identity and value equity as a shared goal, leaders model their own learning, self-disclosing and acknowledging personal biases and fears (Theoharris, 2010). There can be anxiety and fear in offending, appearing angry, or sounding ignorant when discussing issues of race and inequity (Singleton & Hays, 2008). By modeling vulnerability and emphasizing that mistakes will be made when speaking about issues of inequity, leaders can help others overcome those fears and encourage others to take risks in exploring and sharing their own journeys, experiences, and feelings (Sue et al., 2009).

Culturally responsive leaders live this disposition by:

- Demonstrating a belief in eliminating inequities and providing each student with what they need to be successful.
- Openly valuing the diversity of all members of their community.
- Using language that promotes a belief in the ability of each student and adult to achieve, particularly those from groups that have been historically marginalized.
- Modeling vulnerability by acknowledging the work they are doing to become more aware of their own identity, privilege, and biases – and naming their gaps and learning edges related to equity.
- Encouraging risk-taking and creating space for others to have an open dialogue about race, identity, and hard-to-discuss topics.

Possible coaching questions:

- What is your educational vision and philosophy? How do you ensure the community is aware of this vision?
- How is equity integrated and reflected in your school and district's mission and vision statements?
- Which forums do you leverage to share the brilliance of your students and articulate your beliefs about diversity, equity, inclusion, and belonging?
- What are your views on the concept of a growth mindset, and how have you engaged in discussions about mindset with your team?

ACT: Act With Cultural Competence and Responsiveness in Interactions, Decision-Making, and Practice

Racially, culturally, and linguistically diverse students and families experience school differently, making it essential to examine the norms and interactions around race, ethnicity, and diversity within the school environment (Blitz et al., 2020). Equity-centered environments are responsive to and inclusive of the cultural identities of students, staff, and the surrounding community. Leaders play an integral part in developing the school environment and in holding staff accountable for meeting the needs of diverse students and families (Cherkowski, 2010; Khalifa, Gooden, & Davis, 2016). Leaders therefore model culturally responsive practices, including communicating high expectations for all students; designing grade-level, high-quality curriculum that incorporates students' backgrounds, languages, and learning styles; and working with parents and families as valued and respected partners (Gerhart et al., 2011; Klingner et al., 2005; Smith, 2005). Stronger partnerships and collaboration between schools and communities improve family engagement and increase the sense of trust between students, families, and schools (Blitz et al., 2020). It can also reduce cultural misunderstandings and further understanding of the diversity of beliefs and values in the community (Galloway & Ishimaru, 2017; Gordon & Ronder, 2016).

Culturally responsive leaders live this disposition by:

- Actively seeking and making use of diverse perspectives in decision-making.
- Considering the intended and unintended consequences of decisions on all stakeholder groups; in group discussions, paying close attention to which voices aren't being heard and inviting them to express their perspective.
- Cctively seeking to learn about the identities and communities they serve to inform decisions best for them.
- Pushing the decision maker to question which groups are benefiting or being left out when decision are being made, and asking why.
- Engaging in a formal feedback process with all students, families, and community partners regularly.

Possible coaching questions:

- How have your actions and words throughout your career contributed to tackling inequities?
- Could you recount a significant decision you made recently and detail how you ensured that those most affected were involved in the decision-making process?

- Are the decisions you are making as a leader reflecting the needs and priorities of students and families? If so, how? If not, how do you need to change your decision-making process to better reflect the needs of different stakeholders?

BUILD CAPACITY: Purposefully Build the Capacity of Others to Identify and Disrupt Inequities in the School

Culturally responsive work cannot happen in isolation. Without a collaborative effort, staff may believe equity concerns are someone else's job and not their own (Bustamante et al., 2009; Snyder et al., 2019). To ensure members of the learning community both understand and invest in addressing issues of equity and inclusion, leaders build their capacity through collaborative dialogue and professional learning (Galloway & Ishimaru, 2017; Khalifa et al., 2016; Riehl, 2000; Theoharris, 2010). Leaders designate time and space for staff to examine their personal beliefs and collaborate to change educational practice (Alvarez, 2019; Berg, 2018; Gordon & Ronder, 2016; Smith, 2005). They provide time to examine policies for inequities and update them, work with staff democratically, implement shared decision-making structures, and develop a culture of trust and respect. These leaders understand that empowering staff is a key feature of creating more socially just schools (Theoharris, 2010).

Culturally responsive leaders live this disposition by:

- Building others' capacity to learn and practice language and behaviors that are responsive to differences across lines of race, ethnicity, language, class, religion, ability, gender identity and expression, sexual orientation, and other aspects of identity.
- Creating the conditions, common language, and formal structures for regular courageous conversations around equity and culturally responsive practice.
- Providing the space, tools, and support for staff to reflect on their own personal beliefs, biases, assumptions, and behavior, especially those who have been historically minoritized.

- Providing structured and consistent professional learning opportunities to develop and deepen culturally responsive teaching and learning.

Possible coaching questions:

- Who are your accountability partners? How have you created a coalition of leaders around you that push your practice through an equity lens?
- How are you fostering environments that empower others to lead discussions on equity and benefit from constructive feedback from their peers?
- What organizational frameworks have you established to facilitate and promote meaningful, brave dialogues among staff members aimed at benefiting the children and communities you serve?

CONFRONT BIAS: Confront and Alter Institutional Biases of Student Marginalization, Deficit-Based Schooling, and Low Expectations Associated with Minoritized Populations

If schools are to evolve, the organizational structure of schools must be transformed. To do this, leaders must review policies, practices, and structures and remove potential barriers that disadvantage students based on race or ethnicity, gender, ability, sexual orientation, and other characteristics (Bustamante et al., 2009). Students who embody one or many of these characteristics have been minoritized by society and individuals telling them that they are less than and incapable of the skills and abilities of the dominant culture. Confronting these long-standing beliefs and practices requires a collaborative effort, where stakeholders engage in intentional conversations about who benefits from current policy and practice and who is being minoritized or disadvantaged (Klingner et al., 2005). Leaders can initiate the process by examining individual and system data that have been disaggregated by race, ethnicity, and other characteristics; conducting an equity audit; and engaging in a process of collaborative inquiry (Gooden, 2012; Gooden & Dantley, 2012; Larson & Barton, 2013).

Culturally responsive leaders can live this disposition by:

- Taking an inquiry-based approach by asking questions to regularly examine and disaggregate data.
- Confronting behavior that openly or covertly promotes inequity, colorblindness, and deficit thinking.
- Establishing high expectations (performance and behavioral) for adults and students in their school(s), regardless of identity and/or background.
- Engaging in conversations with stakeholders about equity and access, even in the face of risk and pushback.

Possible coaching questions:

- How have you integrated discussions and learning opportunities focused on equity, especially those related to race, into your staff's professional development experiences?
- Reflect on an instance where you recognized and addressed practices or interactions rooted in racial or cultural biases. How did you navigate this challenge, and what were the results?

CREATE SYSTEMS: Create Systems and Structures to Promote Equity with a Focus on Minoritized Populations

Once barriers are identified, leaders must then ensure that new policies and practices are created that prioritize student needs and promote equity (Bustamante et al., 2009). School systems in which all students are successful are systems that create policies based on a thorough analysis of student, teacher, and school data, changing community demographics, and available financial, material, time, and human resources (Klingner et al., 2005). Culturally responsive work is complex, requiring fundamental structural changes and coordinated efforts. Leaders must establish clarity and agreement on a shared vision and plan of action, define clearly articulated measures of success, and build a community-wide commitment to equity and access (Rimmer, 2016). Finally, leaders must ensure that this work is not seen as an add-on but as a lens through which all decisions will be made (Berg, 2018).

Culturally responsive leaders live this disposition by:

- Ensuring that equity is at the forefront of the district and schools' strategic planning process and theories of action.
- Creating processes that promote the recruitment, support, and retention of diverse staff.
- Seeking, allocating, and managing resources to directly support minoritized populations.
- Ensuring that new policies and practices (e.g., curriculum, discipline, funding) prioritize student needs.
- Partnering with families, staff, and communities to ensure fair treatment and equal access to opportunities.

Possible coaching questions:

- How are your recent policies and initiatives, particularly those aimed at teacher recruitment and retention, enhancing the reflection of your student population's diversity within your school or district?
- How do you determine the needs of different groups of students? And then how do you decide how school and district resources are allocated?
- In what ways are you developing your team's ability to share decision-making authority and collaboratively develop a vision with the families and communities you serve?

▶ IDENTITY IS CORE IN LEADERSHIP

Enacting culturally responsive leadership isn't possible without the willingness to include the "whole leader" and the "whole coach" as part of the coaching process, which is why our first equity disposition is *reflect on personal assumptions, beliefs, and behaviors.*

Every person carries with them a unique set of experiences and backgrounds that shape and inform their identity. Woven from threads of race, gender, ethnicity, socioeconomic status, and countless other dimensions, our identities mold how we make meaning of the world, and they inform our interpretations and responses to what we encounter.

There are myriad ways our personal identities and lived experiences shape who we are. They influence how we understand our students and schools and affect the attitudes, behaviors, and decisions that we make. An education leader of color is likely to have experienced systemic and interpersonal racism, gleaning invaluable insights into the hurdles students with similar backgrounds face. Meanwhile, an LGBTQ+ leader might possess an acute sensitivity to the nuances of inclusivity, informed by their own journeys of acceptance and recognition. A leader who immigrated as a child may have encountered some of the same challenges faced by multilingual learning students whose parents struggle to navigate the US education system.

As Honig and Rainey (2023) remind us,

> Principals who support equitable teaching and learning also routinely interrogate and reflect on how their own race, class, gender and other positionalities influence how they lead, and they model for teachers how to do so as part of continuously improving their practice.
>
> (p. 18)

There are a number of strategies to deepen your own and your coachees' understanding of the influence of their identities on their experiences and leadership. Some of these include:

1. **Self-reflection exercises**: Encourage your coachee to engage in self-reflection exercises that prompt them to explore their own identity, experiences, values, and biases. This can be done through journaling, guided questions, or identity-mapping activities.
2. **Identity exploration**: Provide literature or articles that can help them gain insights into how identity influences leadership or suggest workshops and professional learning opportunities on identity and leadership.
3. **Feedback and assessment**: Use self-assessment tools or 360-degree feedback assessments to help your coachee gain insights into how others perceive their leadership behaviors and interactions and the impact of those actions on equity and inclusion.

4. **Case studies**: Share case studies or real-world examples of leaders who have successfully navigated identity-related challenges in their roles.
5. **Role-playing**: Engage in role-playing exercises where your coachee can explore different scenarios and practice navigating identity-related challenges.
6. **Affinity spaces**: Encourage your coachee to seek out affinity groups or networks that can provide opportunities for respite, reflection, and support.

The goal is to cultivate leaders who, with a deeper understanding of their identities, can:

- Modify their leadership techniques to be increasingly inclusive and effective.
- Heighten their understanding of issues of diversity, equity, and inclusion within their leadership environment.
- Design or advocate for policies, practices, and decisions that reflect a commitment to equity, inclusivity, and belonging.
- Cultivate deeper trust and rapport with team members from varied backgrounds, thus enriching communication and collaboration.
- Serve as beacons for students and staff, pioneering a culture where myriad identities are not just recognized but wholeheartedly celebrated.

To help inform your work and measure change over time, we leverage an Equity Leadership Instrument (ELI). This is a self-reflection tool that leaders can use to assess the extent to which their own behaviors reflect the *Equity Leadership Dispositions* necessary to establish equitable schools. In Appendix A, you can find an excerpt from this tool.

In addition, many partner organizations offer powerful tools to support exploration around identity and leadership. Some examples of the resources that are particularly helpful include the National Equity Project's work on Implicit Bias and Structural Inequity, Equity in the Center's Racial Equity Tools repository on Intersectionality, Paul Gorski's Awareness Activities, and the Leadership Circle's Comprehensive 360 Profile Assessment, among many others.

▶ MARCUS AND SARAI'S STORY

In the busy hallways of a high school on Chicago's West Side, timeworn murals of civil rights luminaries and Black poets intersect with a mosaic of lockers – some adorned with graffiti-styled initials, others boasting academic awards. Marcus, a principal serving 14 years as an educator in Chicago's historically Black neighborhoods, sat in his office mourning the loss of 13-year-old Mexican American Adam Toledo, who was killed in the Little Village neighborhood the week prior. Given that Marcus, too, was from the West Side, he wondered about the assumptions and beliefs that adults had about Adam in school and how those assumptions played out in adult interactions and decision-making. He felt personally responsible to elevate a courageous conversation about the Black and Latinx boys they served.

At the staff meeting the following day, Marcus sparked an in-depth, schoolwide conversation about race. It was a vital step toward promoting conversations, understanding, and unity among the diverse student body, where most students were Black or Latinx. Intent on narrowing the experiential divide between faculty and students, he envisioned a school where shared stories and aspirations laid the foundation for genuine understanding and collaboration. As the school principal, Marcus was determined to forge closer connections between the teachers and their students, and most importantly, he wanted to intentionally do his part to ensure that every single student on his campus would be seen, known, and cared for – especially the Black and Latinx boys.

During the staff meeting, the atmosphere was charged with both anticipation and vulnerability. Marcus emphasized the importance of speaking one's truth and taking risks, leveraging Glenn Singleton's norms for courageous conversations (stay engaged, speak your truth, experience discomfort, expect and accept nonclosure). An unexpected moment occurred when a white male teacher, Mr. Johnson, raised his hand to share. With a hint of nervousness in his voice, he revealed a part of his past,

> In my attempt to connect with our students on a deeper level and especially the boys, I tell them how many times I was in central booking when I was a teenager and sometimes I even tell them how many times I have been in jail.

The revelation hung in the air, leaving everyone taken aback, including Marcus. He felt a mix of emotions – discomfort, anger, and a deep sense of empathy. He knew he couldn't ignore such a comment, but he also didn't want to react impulsively and shut down open dialogue. When he later met with his leadership coach, Sarai, he opened up about the situation.

"I feel so disappointed in myself. I called on the next person. I straight up called on the next person," Marcus recounted to his coach, Sarai. She listened intently, sensing the weight of the moment.

"It was an awkward moment. I feel like I should have said something.... That's really what's also bothering me. I feel like it was a missed opportunity to say something," Marcus admitted that thoughts of Adam Toledo, as well as what he personally went through when he was younger, were flashing in his mind during that moment.

Sarai could see the impact of Mr. Johnson's words on Marcus, both as an educator and as a Black man who had also faced his own challenges growing up. She gently probed, "So who were you protecting by not saying anything? Him or you?"

"Both. Me, too. But both.... Well, me primarily. Yeah, probably me," Marcus said, acknowledging his fear of being perceived as an angry or overly emotional Black man in a professional setting.

Sarai held up the proverbial mirror for Marcus, reminding him that his identity matters in leadership; she challenged him to embrace that reality and speak his truth unapologetically. She encouraged him to remember moments when he felt powerful and to draw strength from those memories. She also asked him to reflect on the reason he called the meeting in the first place. "Because I can't stand idle," Marcus shared.

In a subsequent meeting, Marcus decided to address Mr. Johnson's comment head-on. He wanted to understand his perspective fully, knowing that hearing his own experiences might open a path to connection and empathy. Before the meeting, Marcus reached out to Mr. Johnson privately to have a candid conversation and prep him for the next staff meeting.

As he stood in front of the staff, Marcus shared more about his own experiences growing up. He spoke about how triggering the murder of Adam Toledo was for him, as it reminded him of the many challenges and struggles he faced, including a moment from his past when he was unjustly arrested as a teenager. He revealed how being arrested traumatized him and shaped his worldview and the empathy he felt toward his students' struggles.

> Last week, Mr. Johnson made a statement that bothered me as a person of color. It made me think that your belief was that the way you could connect to Black and Latinx students would be talking about jail, and that made me wonder about your beliefs about young men of color.

Marcus addressed the issue directly, his voice firm yet compassionate.

He continued, "As we continue in this work, I really think it's important for all of us to be reminded that we may say things that offend each other in this space. We can model grace and empathy, but we can't move it forward as a community unless we start to challenge each other's thinking, and the only way to do that is through speaking our truth."

In that defining moment in the story, Marcus embodied culturally responsive leadership, speaking from the heart and advocating for his students' well-being. He demonstrated the courage to confront bias and lead by example, encouraging his staff to do the same.

The journey toward becoming an exceptional leader and fostering meaningful connections was in progress. Through embracing his identity as a Black educator, he realized the power of vulnerability and empathy, ultimately strengthening the bond with his staff and students alike.

This transformative experience was not merely the result of innate intuition or spur-of-the-moment decision-making, but rather, it evolved through facilitative coaching and thoughtful reflection.

Behind the scenes, the underpinnings of a robust and structured coaching relationship with Sarai were at play. Such partnerships aren't forged overnight; they require mutual trust, respect, vulnerability, and a clear understanding of the desired outcomes. They also include both the coach's and coachee's courage and willingness to talk about race and identity and how it shows up in leadership.

▶ COACHING ALONG THE DIMENSIONS

As a culturally responsive leader or coach, you cannot separate who you are as a leader or as a coach from the person you are, the lived experiences you've encountered, and the values you hold. Moving forward, the six dispositions could serve as a toolbox for Coach Sarai to continue coaching Marcus. Here are some examples of the types of questions she might ask:

1. *REFLECT*: Reflect on personal assumptions, beliefs, and behaviors.
    - What are your own beliefs and biases about Black and Latinx young men?
    - Where do you think these beliefs came from, and what do you need to learn or unlearn?
2. *MODEL BELIEFS*: Publicly model a personal belief system that is grounded in equity.
    - How will you continue to demonstrate what it looks like to engage with students in a way that makes them feel seen, known, and cared for?
    - How do your beliefs show up in the expectations you have around instruction?

3. *ACT*: Act with cultural competence and responsiveness in interactions, decision-making, and practice.
   - How are you personally interrupting the pattern that one in four Latinx/Black neurodiverse students experience at least one out-of-school suspension?
   - How are you ensuring that your decisions are asset-based and restorative, as opposed to deficit-based and punitive?
4. *BUILD CAPACITY*: Purposefully build the capacity of others to identify and disrupt inequities in the school
   - How are you building the capacity of staff members struggling to meet the needs of students?
   - How will you support Mr. Johnson in unpacking his assumptions?
   - Where are you providing adequate support for the students who need it most?
5. *CONFRONT BIAS*: Confront and alter institutional biases of student marginalization, deficit-based schooling, and low expectations associated with minoritized populations.
   - How are you confronting deficit-based beliefs in real time? What processes and/or systems are in place?
6. *CREATE SYSTEMS*: Create systems and structures to promote equity with a focus on minoritized populations.
   - What are you doing, and what can you do to address the glaring disparities your data has revealed in a systemic, sustainable way?

▶ FINAL THOUGHTS

Developing self-awareness lays a strong foundation for enacting culturally responsive leadership, but it doesn't end there. The ability for school and system leaders to grow more attuned to the diverse needs of their student body, lead more equitable practices and policies, and create educational spaces that truly center all students is not possible without an investment in the whole leader.

BACK TO YOU

- Why was it so important for Marcus to reflect on his own identity or discuss his personal experiences with his staff? Consider how elevating conversations about race and the intersections of identity can be beneficial to your coachee. *Engage your coachee in one of the strategies from this chapter to support self-reflection and identity exploration.*
- To what extent do you embody these six *Equity Leadership Dispositions* in your leadership practice? *Pick one disposition that is a growth area for you and consider how to respond to the implications that surface when you explore the reflection questions.*
- How can you use the six *Equity Leadership Dispositions* with your current coachees to build their cultural competence? *Identify one disposition that represents a growth area for your coachee and determine what questions you may want to ask or what coaching activity you want to engage them in during the next coaching session.*
- What aspects of your own identity do you typically share with your coachees? What do you choose to keep to yourself? Why? *If there are any aspects you should start or stop sharing, commit yourself to changing what you share.*
- In what ways, if any, is your coaching different when you are working with someone who shares similar aspects of identity than when you are working with someone who doesn't? *Think about how this impacts your coaching.*

Bibliography

Alvarez, A. (2019). Confronting inequity/teacher leadership for equity. *Educational Leadership*, *76*(6). https://www.ascd.org/el/articles/teacher-leadership-for-equity

Berg, J. H. (2018). Educating ourselves for equity. *Educational Leadership*, *76*(3). https://www.ascd.org/el/articles/educating-ourselves-for-equity

Blitz, L. V., Yull, D., & Clauhs, M. (2020). Bringing sanctuary to school: Assessing school climate as a foundation for culturally responsive trauma-informed approaches for urban schools. *Urban Education*, *55*(1) 95–124.

Brooks, J. S., Jean-Marie, G., Normore, A., & Hodgins, D. (2007). Distributed leadership for social justice: Exploring how influence and equity are stretched over an urban high school. *Journal of School Leadership*, *17*(4), 378–408.

Brown, K. M. (2004). Leadership for social justice and equity: Weaving a transformative framework and pedagogy. *Educational Administration Quarterly*, *40*(1), 77–108.

Bustamante, R. M., Nelson, J. A., & Onwuegbuzie, A. J. (2009). Assessing schoolwide cultural competence: Implications for school leadership preparation. *Educational Administration*, *45*, 793–827.

Cherkowski, S. (2010). Leadership for diversity, inclusion and sustainability: Teachers as leaders. *Citizenship, Social and Economics Education*, *9*(1), 23–31.

Fabina, J., Hernandez, E., & McElrath, K. (2021). *School enrollment in the United States: 2021*. United States Census Bureau. https://www.census.gov/content/dam/Census/library/publications/2023/acs/acs-55.pdf

Frey, W. (2021). *New 2020 census results show increased diversity countering decade-long declines in America's white and youth populations*. Brookings Institution. https://www.brookings.edu/articles/new-2020-census-results-show-increased-diversity-countering-decade-long-declines-in-americas-white-and-youth-populations/

Galloway, M. K., & Ishimaru, A. M. (2017). Equitable leadership on the ground: Converging on high-leverage practices. *Education Policy Analysis Archives*, *25*(2), 1–36.

Gerhart, L. G., Harris, S., & Mixon, J. (2011). Beliefs and effective practices of successful principals in high schools with an Hispanic population of at least 30%. *NASSP Bulletin, 95*(4), 266–280.

Gooden, M. A. (2012). What does racism have to do with leadership? Countering the idea of color-blind leadership: A reflection on race and the growing pressures of the urban principalship. *The Journal of Educational Foundations, 26*(1/2), 67–84.

Gooden, M. A., & Dantley, M. (2012). Centering race in a framework for leadership preparation. *Journal of Research on Leadership Education, 7*(2), 237–253.

Gooden, M. A., & O'Doherty, A. (2015). Do you see what I see? Fostering aspiring leaders racial awareness. *Urban Education, 50*(2), 225–255.

Gordon, S. P., & Ronder, E. A. (2016). Perceptions of culturally responsive leadership inside and outside of a principal preparation program. *International Journal of Educational Reform, 25*(2), 125–153.

Grissom, J. A., Egalite, A. J., & Lindsay, C. A. (2021). *How principals affect students and schools: A systematic synthesis of two decades of research.* The Wallace Foundation. https://wallacefoundation.org/report/how-principals-affect-students-and-schools-systematic-synthesis-two-decades-research

Honig, M., & Rainey, L. (2023). *From tinkering to transformation: How school district central offices drive teaching and learning.* Harvard Education Press.

Jones, S., & Vagule, M. D. (2013). Living contradictions and working for change: Toward a theory of class-sensitive pedagogy. *Educational Researcher, 42*(3), 129–141.

Khalifa, M. A., Gooden, M. A., & Davis, J. E. (2016). Culturally responsive school leadership: A synthesis of the literature. *Review of Educational Research, 86*(4), 1272–1311.

Klingner, J. K., Artiles, A. J., Kozleski, E., Harry, B., Zion, S., & Tate, W. (2005). Addressing the disproportionate representation of culturally and linguistically diverse students in special education through culturally responsive educational systems. *Education Policy Analysis Archives, 13*(38), 1–40.

Krogstad, J. (2019). A view of the nation's future through Kindergarten Demographics. Pew Research Center. https://www.pewresearch.org/short-reads/2019/07/31/kindergarten-demographics-in-us/

Larson, R., & Barton, R. (2013). Lessons on leading for equity. *Principal Leadership, 13*(8), 19–24.

Nelson, S. W., & Guerra, P. L. (2014). Educator beliefs and cultural knowledge: Implications for school improvement efforts. *Educational Administration Quarterly, 50*(1), 67–95.

Riehl, C. L. (2000). The principal's role in creating inclusive schools for diverse students: A review of normative, empirical, and critical literature on the practice of educational administration. *Review of Educational Research, 70*(1), 55–81.

Rigby, J.G., & Tredway, L. (2015). Actions matter: How school leaders enact equity principles. In M. Khalifa; A. Noelle Witherspoon; A. F. Osanloo, & C. M. Grant (Eds.), *Handbook of urban educational leadership.* Rowman & Littlefield Publishers.

Rimmer, J. (2016). Developing principals as equity-centered instructional leaders. In *Equity-centered capacity building: Essential approaches for excellence & sustainable school system transformation* (pp. 93–106). The Equity-Centered Capacity Building Network. https://capacitybuildingnetwork.org/article9/

Ross, J. A., & Berger, M.-J. (2009). Equity and leadership: Research-based strategies for school leaders. *School Leadership and Management, 29*(5), 461–474.

Singleton, G. (2014). *Courageous conversations about race: A field guide for achieving equity in schools.* Corwin.

Singleton, G. E., & Hays, C. (2008). Beginning courageous conversations about race. In M. Pollock (Ed.), *Everyday antiracism: Getting real about race in school.* The New Press.

Smith, C. A. (2005). School factors that contribute to the underachievement of students of color and what culturally competent school leaders can do. *Education Leadership and Administration, 17,* 21–32.

Snyder, A., Trowery, L., & McGrath, K. (2019). *Guiding principles for equity in education.* McGraw Hill.

Sue, D. W., Torino, G. C., Campodilupo, C. M., Rivera, D. P., & Lin, A. I. (2009). How white faculty perceive and react to difficult dialogues on race: Implications for education and training. *The Counseling Psychologist, 37*(8), 1090–1115.

The Leadership Academy. (2022). *Equity leadership dispositions.* https://www.leadershipacademy.org/wp-content/uploads/2020/11/Rebrand-Version-Equity-Leadership-Dispositions.pdf

The Leadership Academy. (2024). *Portrait of a culturally responsive system.* https://www.leadershipacademy.org/resources/portrait-of-a-culturally-responsive-school-system-2/

Theoharris, G. (2010). Disrupting injustice: Principals narrate the strategies they use to improve their schools and advance social justice. *Teachers College Record, 112*(1), 331–373.

Yasharian, F. (January 9, 2019). Uncomfortable by design: Learning and leading with the support of a coach. *Leadership insights.* https://www.leadershipacademy.org/blog/uncomfortable-by-design/

Initiating the Coaching Relationship

Chapter 3

> *"People look to you to solve their problems but, when you take a coaching stance, you're empowering them to solve their own problems and build their skill set to see problems from multiple perspectives and explore new possibilities for action."*
>
> – Coach, The Leadership Academy

BIG IDEAS IN THIS CHAPTER

- To demystify any preconceived notions about coaching and to establish a strong foundation for your coaching relationship, it is important to come to a shared agreement on the purpose and to establish norms for your work together.
- Goal setting provides a road map for coachees to achieve success and drive meaningful transformational change within their schools and systems. This chapter outlines six key practices to guide the goal-setting process.
- Recognizing and proactively addressing disengagement can get a coaching relationship on track.

As you embark on a new coaching relationship, there are essential steps you should undertake to establish a strong foundation. At the outset, it is imperative that you develop a shared understanding of the purpose of *Facilitative Competency-Based (FCB) Coaching*. Once that initial base is set, you can collaboratively set agreements to maximize learning and pave the way for clear communication. As your partnership begins to build, the next step is to determine the goals for impact that will set the direction for your work together. Last but not least, be vigilant in checking for and addressing cracks in the foundation, which may manifest as disengagement on the part of your coachee. In this chapter, we will explore each of these steps in turn.

▶ STEP 1: ESTABLISH A SHARED UNDERSTANDING OF THE PURPOSE OF FCB COACHING

Numerous coaching models exist, and both you and your coachee likely bring diverse experiences and assumptions about coaching to the table. These prior influences can significantly shape your expectations upon entering into the coaching relationship, so it is of paramount importance that you examine any preconceived notions and establish, right from the start, a clear and explicit understanding of what FCB Coaching means and its ultimate purpose.

At The Leadership Academy, we define FCB Coaching as creating an environment in which the education leader engages in critical and targeted reflection on their practice as it relates to the competencies. The ultimate goal is facilitating the paradigm or behavioral shifts necessary for culturally responsive leadership. This enables the leader to build systems and structures to promote equity and purposefully develop the capacity of their staff to ensure students have all they need to achieve academic, social, and emotional success.

In describing what coaching is about, it's important to be clear about what coaching is NOT.

- Coaching is **not** about directing the coachee to take certain actions.

- Coaching is **not** a punitive requirement or an intervention for poor performance.
- Coaching is **not** about being a friend who talks to the coachee about whatever is on their mind.
- Coaching is **not** about inspiring coachees to be replicas of their coach.

Rather, coaching is about implicating leaders in the system of instructional improvement and building the habits of reflective practice and capacity for the adaptive leadership necessary to change outcomes for students. Coaching compels leaders to imagine what success looks like for them and to take ownership of challenging inequities.

▶ STEP 2: SET AGREEMENTS TO MAXIMIZE LEARNING AND DEVELOPMENT

Before diving deep into the intricacies of a coaching relationship, it is crucial to recognize the foundational role that norm-setting plays. Norms are a clear set of agreements about how to work best together. As the bedrock of productive and respectful interactions, they function as a guiding compass, ensuring that both coach and coachee are aligned in their intentions and approaches.

Setting norms together at the beginning of a coaching relationship helps to establish clarity and define expectations for engagement. Shared agreements build trust, promote open communication, create accountability, and allow for individual adjustments as needed.

We suggest you put norms in writing so you can revisit them from time to time. The following are common expectations in the coaching relationship and what they entail for each role. You can use these norms as a starting point for your discussion and prompt your coachee to articulate what they need in place in order to experience success. You can ask questions like: "What other norms or agreements do we need?" Or, "How can our coaching engagement be structured to best support or advance this work?"

Initiating the Coaching Relationship 53

	Recommended Coaching Expectations	
	Coach	Coachee
Clarity of Purpose	Brings a commitment to working closely with the leader to assess areas for growth and development for both the leader and the school and system. Focuses on advancing the leader's goals, strengthening the coachee's leadership competencies—and practice as a culturally responsive leader—and supports them in building organizational capacity and improving instructional quality on behalf of all students. Consistently brings a culturally responsive lens to the work. Respects the coachee and commits to learning from the relationship.	Commits to prioritizing their own leadership development and to identify areas for growth on behalf of the school and system community. Demonstrates mutual respect and intention to learn from the coaching experience.
Reliability and Preparation	Schedules regular ongoing conversations, interactions, and coaching sessions designed to address development goals.	Helps schedule and prepare for sessions and makes a time commitment to the coaching relationship.
Openness, Trust, and Confidentiality	Pushes the leader's thinking in service of learning even when doing so may create discomfort. The coach is receptive to the leader's feedback regarding the coaching relationship and is willing to modify strategies and approaches. Maintains discretion and confidentiality within the boundaries defined and agreed to by both coach and coachee.	Has an openness and willingness to provide the coach with candid and timely feedback regarding the coaching relationship. Commits to honesty and to taking measured risks, including doing what may feel uncomfortable, in order to learn and expand leadership capacity.

(Continued)

	Recommended Coaching Expectations	
	Coach	Coachee
Customized Support	Individualizes support that addresses the leader's specific leadership needs and context as aligned to system priorities.	Collaborates with the coach to identify goals and evaluate achievement of goals.
Feedback	Offers timely and candid feedback on leadership practices to help the leader grow their capacity to improve teaching and learning for all students. Asks for honest, real-time feedback from the coachee in order to improve the relationship and their practice.	Commits to being receptive to feedback—a willingness to receive feedback regarding their leadership practices so that they can reach their goals while understanding that there may be moments of productive discomfort in service of learning. Provides direct and honest feedback to the coach about how they are experiencing the coaching engagement.

▶ AN ADDITIONAL NOTE ON CONFIDENTIALITY

Ideally, coaching creates the space for education leaders. They should freely engage in learning without having to worry about repercussions of revealing vulnerabilities or challenges. Talk together about what is and isn't confidential and what confidentiality means to each of you. Define and ensure terms of confidentiality with the education leader and their organization.

▶ STEP 3: AGREE UPON BASIC LOGISTICS

While it may not be the most interesting part of your conversation, confirming basic logistics and technical details with your coachee will be key to ensuring clear communication channels leading up to, in-between, and after coaching sessions.

Sample Coaching Logistics Prompts
- What's the best phone number and email address for you? And your assistant (if applicable)?
- How will we schedule coaching sessions? What's the best way for us to schedule our sessions?
- What are the best ways to communicate with each other? Will coaching be in person, over the phone, virtual, or a mix of modalities? What are your hours of availability for calls/texts? (Mutually decide on the type of meeting: length of meeting, phone call, video conference, collaborative document share, on camera, etc.). Where can we meet privately for in-person visits?
- What should be the frequency and duration of coaching sessions? (Establish a preferred frequency for communications and meetings to set a rhythm for the relationship. Vary the meeting time so the coachee can participate during their best time given personal and professional demands.)
- How many hours of coaching should the leader expect to receive? What is the start and end date of the engagement?
- What should be the process for canceling coaching sessions? (Be sure to discuss with your coachee if there is a specific cancellation policy in place.)

▶ STEP 4: DETERMINE GOALS FOR IMPACT

Goal setting provides a roadmap for coachees to achieve success and drive meaningful change within their schools or systems. You will set goals with your coachee as part of your foundational sessions together. To ensure the effectiveness of goal setting, several key components must be considered. One component is aligning goals with the leader's system-level priorities and organizational context. Another component is creating the conditions in which the coachee can identify their growth areas and envision progress. Do your due diligence and familiarize yourself with the coachee's broader school, community, and system context. Here are six "Do's" or suggested practices for the coach and coachee to engage in together when determining goals:

✓ **Do connect to system-level priorities**: Align goals with the broader organizational context, objectives, and strategic initiatives.

One essential question to consider when identifying goals is:

- *What is the leader going to be held accountable for in the short and long term?*

Take, for instance, a system prioritizing an initiative around adopting a uniform literacy curriculum. It would be imperative for the coach and leader to consider what shifts need to take place in the school for the curricula to be implemented successfully, as well as what the leader needs to work on personally in order to successfully fulfill that mandate. By intentionally attending to the system-level priorities and organizational context, the coach and coachee are minimizing the potential for misalignment and lack of impact.

When a coach focuses solely on the personal leadership development goals of the coachee without addressing systemic issues, they may inadvertently limit the coachee's broader influence and potential for sustainable change. Addressing system-level priorities ensures that the goals have a ripple effect, creating positive shifts not just for the individual leader but for the entire organization and, most importantly, for every student – in other words, developing *self* in service of the *system*. Furthermore, by tackling systemic issues, the coachee can address root causes rather than just symptoms, leading to more profound, lasting transformation. This holistic approach also solidifies the leader's role as an agent of change, reinforcing their position within the system and amplifying their ability to drive meaningful, long-term results.

For example, Roberta, a principal of a high school with decreasing attendance, initially set a goal to improve her school's extracurricular and community events, thinking this would encourage student participation and engagement at school. However, after discussing the district's priority to reduce absenteeism with her coach, she realized a more aligned approach was needed and shifted her focus. She made a goal to hold regular communication sessions with key staff and parents to understand the root causes of her students' absences, and she set another goal to improve collaboration and communication among her teachers and social workers by reshaping the school's teaming structure. These moves enabled her staff to collaborate more effectively around addressing students' academic and personal challenges, and the school made significant strides in reducing absenteeism, proving the value of tying goals closely to system-level objectives.

> ✓ **Do align with existing parameters**: Ensure that the goals align with the leader's current goal-setting or evaluation system.

Another set of important questions to answer at the onset of the goal-setting process is as follows:

- *How will the leader be evaluated?*
- *What leadership framework/model does the system utilize to identify what leaders need to know and be able to do?*

Effective coaches will make sure that the goal-setting process operates within the existing set of leadership competencies or performance standards of the coachee's role, e.g., Professional Standards for Education Leaders (PSEL) or the Council of Chief State School Officer's Model Principal Supervisor Professional Standards. This ensures that the coaching approach does not result in disjointed or additional goals that are outside the parameters of the existing evaluation system but rather are embedded and enhance the leadership development efforts already in place. If a school already has a comprehensive teacher evaluation process, setting additional and duplicative goals outside of that process can create confusion and undermine the existing system.

For example, Braxton, an elementary school principal who was already struggling with a comprehensive teacher evaluation process in her school, felt overwhelmed and confused when her coach proposed an entirely new set of criteria. Instead of streamlining her objectives, the addition created chaos and diminished the effectiveness of both the old and the new systems. Recognizing this, her coach regrouped, ensuring that the new goal-setting process dovetailed with the school's existing leadership competencies, in this case within the context of PSEL. By doing so, they managed to create a unified and cohesive plan, reinforcing

Braxton's leadership without overburdening her. This is a testament to the importance of ensuring that coaching does not introduce disjointed goals but rather complements and enhances ongoing leadership development efforts.

> ✓ **Do gauge current practice and capacity**: Develop a comprehensive understanding of the leader's current practices and skill set to identify priorities and points of leverage.

When determining goals with a coachee, it is also vital to understand their current capacity. Knowing where they are in relation to where they need to be can illuminate various pathways toward achieving their goals. Begin by assessing the leader's existing skills and practices. This initial step is crucial in setting a baseline that can spotlight areas for growth and determine the next steps.

Here are some questions to explore with your coachee:

- *What will making the organizational shifts require of you in terms of your leadership?*
- *To what extent are you already exhibiting the necessary leadership actions?*
- *In what ways can you leverage your strengths? How might you need to address areas for improvement?*

It is important for you to get to know the leader's current capabilities since goals that don't account for their starting point can be unrealistic and lead to disengagement.

For example, consider the experience of Melanie, a principal who took charge of Westridge Elementary at a time when the school district was encouraging schools to leverage digital tools for both administrative tasks and classroom instruction. Melanie, with her traditional teaching background, had always been more of a pen-and-paper administrator, although she acknowledged the benefits of technological advancements in education. In their initial coaching sessions, her coach, Avi, observed Melanie's apprehension when discussing technology. Instead of delving deep into digital strategy, Avi chose to first understand Melanie's comfort level. They discovered that Melanie had once attempted to introduce an online student assessment tool but faced resistance from the teaching staff, who were not adequately trained, and from parents, who felt left in the dark.

Recognizing Melanie's foundational level and past experiences, Avi decided to adopt a gradual step-by-step approach. First, they set a goal to introduce Melanie to an educational management software tailored for beginners. The next steps involved structured training sessions for both Melanie and her teaching staff, alongside a robust communication plan to keep parents informed.

Over time, Melanie became more confident with digital tools, allowing for the setting of more ambitious technological integration goals for Westridge Elementary. By acknowledging her starting point and past experiences, Avi was able to craft a plan that matched her pace and ensured success.

- ✓ **Do envision success and identify shifts**: Encourage leaders to imagine what goal attainment might look like and identify the mindsets and behaviors that could contribute to and/or hinder advancement.

Superimposing your own definition of success can lead to unmet expectations and frustration for both you and your coachee. It is of utmost importance that you help your coachee envision what success would look, sound, and feel like for them in their unique context. As part of this exploration, you can support them in considering how their thinking and behaviors might need to shift.

Some questions you can ask are:

- *Let's imagine 6–12 months from now that you are successful in the things within your sphere of influence and locus of control. What are the three things you have done?*
- *What are the underlying assumptions at play in terms of how you are thinking about this?*
- *What mindsets might be getting in your way as you determine a path forward?*
- *What behaviors would best enable you to make progress toward your goal?*
- *What might you need to stop, start, and/or continue doing in order to achieve your goals?*

Mindset and behavior shifts are critical for goal attainment (Dweck, 2006). For example, if a leader needs to improve their collaboration skills, simply setting a goal without addressing any underlying mindset or behavior changes may limit their progress.

For example, imagine Fred, a middle school principal who was determined to foster a more inclusive school environment where every student, every background, felt valued and heard. During a coaching session, Fred's coach helped him to realize that, while his intent was clear, he had ingrained behaviors and mindsets that acted as barriers. With the coach's guidance, Fred pinpointed a goal that involved a mindset shift: from seeing inclusivity as an added task to viewing it as an integral component of every school activity. This translated into a behavioral change where he began initiating monthly roundtable discussions with students from diverse backgrounds, listening to their experiences, and integrating their feedback into school policies. The shift wasn't just about hosting discussions; it was about genuinely valuing the voices and ensuring they played a role in shaping the school's future.

> ✓ **Do promote equitable and culturally responsive practices**: Explicitly mention the intended impact on equitable or culturally responsive practices. Keep students at the center of the work.

While leadership coaching results in the coachee becoming a better version of themselves, this is not an end in itself. The leader's growth or improvement is not solely a self-seeking endeavor. Culturally responsive leadership at its core is on behalf of children and families and should catalyze impact at a systemic level.

Here are a few prompts that can help you and your coachee remain anchored to the ultimate purpose:

- *In what ways will students, especially those who have been historically minoritized, benefit?*
- *What will be different for children and/or their families if the goal is met?*

For example, Elandria, principal of Eastwood High School in Brooklyn, was grappling with the concern that her Multilingual Learner students (MLLs), many of whom come from immigrant families, were performing below average in standardized assessments. With the guidance of her leadership coach, Carlos, they embarked on a deep dive to understand the underlying factors.

Carlos started by prompting Elandria: "In what ways are the current instructional practices aligning or not aligning with the cultural and linguistic backgrounds of these students?" This question led Elandria to a revelation: The majority of teaching resources used were not culturally relevant to the MLLs, leading to a lack of engagement and connection.

Together, they set a goal to integrate culturally responsive teaching materials into the English Language Arts (ELA) and Math curriculum. Carlos then posed the next question, "What will be different for these students and their families if this goal is met?" Elandria reflected and realized that not only were the students likely to perform better academically, but they were also likely to feel better seen and represented in their learning environment. This inclusion could help to boost students' self-esteem, engagement, and sense of belonging in the school community.

Additionally, Elandria decided to host monthly community meetings with translators present to involve parents in the decision-making process and gather feedback on the newly implemented teaching resources. The aim was to foster a deeper school-community relationship and ensure that the needs of the multilingual students were holistically met.

Months into the initiative, not only have the MLLs' test scores improved, but there's a noticeable boost in their participation in class and extracurricular activities. Parents, now more involved, express gratitude for being engaged as active stakeholders in their children's education.

The ripple effect of embedding equitable and culturally responsive practices into school leadership goals can be profound for the coachee and for every student in their school or community. By focusing on the unique needs of a specific student group, Eastwood High didn't just improve test scores but also enriched the overall school experience for these students and their families.

- ✓ **Do craft a systematic approach to monitoring and measuring impact**: Create a plan to periodically gather evidence, assess progress, and course correct.

An effective goal-setting approach incorporates an accountability process to monitor and measure impact in a timely manner that allows for informed adjustments.

The fundamental questions for the coach and leader to explore are:

- *How will success and impact be defined, and in what ways can it be measured?*
- *How will we know that the shifts we are making are reaping the intended benefits for children and families?*
- *By what means and in what time frames will we assess progress toward goals? How will we assess the actual versus intended outcomes?*

For example, Antonia, a principal at an elementary school in Boston, and her leadership coach, Steven, decided to address the school's declining reading levels among their third-grade students. They realized that setting a vague goal like "improving reading levels" wouldn't suffice. Instead, they decided on a clear and specific objective: "Increase the percentage of third graders reading at grade level by 15 percent by the end of the academic year."

To systematically monitor and measure the impact of their efforts, Antonia and Steven undertook the following steps:

- **Defining success**: A successful outcome would be realized when 85% of the third-grade students could read at or above grade level by the end of the academic year.
- **Developing a measurement strategy**: Monthly formative assessments would be conducted using standardized tools to gauge reading proficiency and comprehension. This would offer a clear, quantitative measure of progress.
- **Creating a feedback loop**: Teachers were encouraged to share qualitative feedback on individual students' progress during biweekly staff meetings. This would allow for more nuanced understandings and early identification of those needing additional support.

- **Evaluating outcomes and inputs**: By comparing the outcomes (reading proficiency) with the inputs (resources like additional reading hours, teacher training workshops, and remedial classes), they could ensure the resources deployed were effective and meeting targets.
- **Making informed adjustments**: Six months into the initiative, their regular assessments revealed that only 8 percent improvement had been achieved. Armed with this evidence, Antonia and Steven course-corrected by implementing an after-school reading program and inviting local community volunteers to assist.

Their systematic approach to monitoring and measuring impact ensured that they remained proactive and agile, continually aligning their strategies to best serve the children's learning needs.

Imagine goal setting as placing a pebble in a pond. The splash is immediate and localized, but the ripples it creates touch every part of the water. Similarly, each goal set by a leader sends currents through the broader system. Stay attuned to interconnections and underlying dynamics so you can support your coachee in crafting goals that not only address immediate challenges but also affect meaningful, systemic change on behalf of children and families. When you integrate these six "dos" or best practices of goal setting, you and your coachee will be able to collaboratively devise objectives that not only match organizational aspirations but also initiate profound transformation. See Appendix B for a workbook you can utilize to plan and co-develop goal(s) with your coachee.

▶ STEP 5: ADDRESS DISENGAGEMENT DIRECTLY

As a coach, you must also pay attention to the power dynamics that set the stage for your relationships with your coachees – particularly in educational institutions, where a leader might feel "voluntold" into the coaching relationship. Coaching can be imposed as part of a district's turnaround effort, for example, and when it is perceived by the school leader as a punitive or evaluative measure, power dynamics play an even more critical role. At other times, a breach of trust or conflict between you and your coachee can emerge, creating discomfort or hesitance in the coaching relationship. If you're positioned as a coach and feel a hint of unease from your coachee, it is important to initiate an open dialogue right away. Don't wait for it to grow into detachment or disinterest.

For example, Martha, with 15 years of coaching under her belt, remembered her sessions with Jim. "I was surprised when Jim chose me as his coach," Martha said, "The deputy chancellor had mentioned that everyone gets a coach, but Jim's involvement always felt more like he was meeting a requirement." Jim was a high-ranking officer in a high-poverty district in New York City and not an easy character to get to know. He was undeniably talented and exuded a quiet confidence, but Martha sensed an underlying hesitance. "Our sessions felt a bit like a dance, with Jim always maintaining a safe distance."

One day, Martha joined Jim on a visit to a school in his district. Engaging with the principal, she was immersed in the day-to-day concerns and challenges the school faced. When she later discussed these observations with Jim, she noticed his immediate reflex to problem-solve, often without fully digesting the issue at hand.

Their next coaching session felt pivotal. Martha, choosing her words carefully, began, "Jim, I feel there's a layer we haven't yet uncovered. I realize that in a position like yours, especially leading some of the most challenging schools in the district, there's a natural instinct to protect oneself. But I genuinely want to help, not hinder your work here."

Jim's eyes widened slightly, perhaps not anticipating Martha's directness. After a moment's reflection, he replied, "Martha, in my role, vulnerability can be costly. But it's not just about me. I have a team, students, and a community relying on my decisions." Martha nodded, "I completely understand, Jim. But remember, growth often starts with recognizing areas of development. I'm here to be a sounding board, to offer strategies, not to critique or report."

There was a moment of silence before Jim responded, his voice tinged with emotion, "I've always been in a position where

I had to guard myself. It's refreshing, but a bit scary, to think I might not have to."

From that point on, their sessions took a turn. Jim began sharing more openly about his challenges. The walls he had built began to crumble, and as trust grew, so did their collaboration, leading to some significant changes in his leadership practices and eventually to improvements in the schools in his district.

One key insight that Martha's experience underscores is the importance of recognizing and addressing disengagement directly. One of The Leadership Academy's coaches put it this way. "The first thing is naming the resistance. 'I feel resistance.'" Even if it's on your end, you need to vocalize it.

Face the unspoken tensions head-on, utilizing language that prepares your coachee for what might be a challenging conversation. For example:

- *I'm about to share feedback that might be hard to hear.*
- *I sense resistance from you. Can we discuss it?*
- *There seems to be a reluctance to engage or an unwillingness to answer the question. What is happening for you when we broach this topic? What can we do to talk this through?*

Make it abundantly clear that you recognize the potential discomfort of the dynamic. When appropriate, assure your coachees that your discussions are confidential and your role is that of a supporter and collaborator, not a judge, critic, or evaluator. Directly and candidly confronting these dynamics is the best way to pave the path toward trust.

▶ FINAL THOUGHTS

Coaching is more than just a developmental tool; it's a catalyst for change, a force for equity, and a pathway to more inclusive educational environments. FCB Coaching is designed to nurture and challenge educational leaders, encouraging them to confront systemic inequities and fostering the conditions for all students, especially those historically marginalized, to thrive. To do this hard work, effective coaching necessitates an authentic partnership between the coach and coachee, enabling them to collaboratively establish the boundaries and goals of their engagement. In this chapter, we have explored the practical aspects of launching a successful coaching relationship. As we move forward, we will delve more deeply into the strategies, tools, and techniques that can further enhance the coaching journey, supporting education leaders to reach their learning edge in their quest for growth, equity, and improved outcomes for all students.

> **BACK TO YOU**
>
> - How might you and your coachee develop and recalibrate your agreements to maximize learning and development? *In your next coaching session, ask your coachee what you individually and jointly need to stop, start, and continue doing.*
> - In what ways can you refine or enhance existing coaching goals based on the goal-setting strategies? *Use the questions from the "Do's" in this chapter to audit existing goals and surface timely adjustments to maximize learning and impact.*
> - What, if any, forms of disengagement have you encountered in your coaching experience? What moves have you made to turn things around? What other approaches might you consider using in future situations? *Try out a new approach when the need next arises.*
> - Are there any current situations in which you feel you and your coachee are "dancing around" an issue or feeling? *Practice what you would say as part of a more direct conversation.*

Bibliography

Dweck, C. (2006). *Mindset: The new psychology of success.* Random House.
Senge, P. (2006). *The fifth discipline.* Random House Business.

Chapter 4: Creating the Conditions to Go Deep

> **❝**For me, it's listening for the voice inflection, it's looking for the twinkle in someone's eyes. I am looking for where the excitement comes from when they're talking, or when they're sharing about who they are and their journey. I am paying attention to those things, not just in our introductory meetings, but throughout our work together because it gives me insight and enlightenment regarding what their passion is and what they value the most. That helps me tap into what drives them and motivates them so I can make coaching as impactful and beneficial as it can be.**❞**
>
> – Coach, The Leadership Academy

BIG IDEAS IN THIS CHAPTER

- Conditions that allow for a deeper level of learning include a trusting relationship, a focus on meaning-making, adopting an inquiry stance, tailoring support, and respecting boundaries.
- Trust is not built *before* coaching, it is built *by* coaching with care, competence, reliability, and sincerity.
- Helping leaders understand and see the patterns in their own meaning-making creates the space for them to challenge their assumptions, reflect on their impact, and explore new approaches.
- Adopting an inquiry stance is essential to asking effective questions that are purposeful and generative.
- Understanding how your coachee thinks and learns allows you to tailor your sessions and meet their specific learning needs.

Facilitative Competency Based (FCB) Coaching Coaching is not for the faint of heart. It demands that coachees reckon with themselves and grapple with the implications of their beliefs, behaviors, and actions as they grow into culturally responsive leaders. Coaches can intentionally create the conditions for this leadership growth to occur by building trust, tailoring their approach, and supporting their coachees in developing greater self-awareness and a better understanding of their own assumptions and meaning-making.

▶ FIND YOUR WAY TO THE KITCHEN!

Trust is the bedrock of all genuine human relationships. It's the intangible bridge that connects two people and allows for deeper understanding, more effective communication, and impactful growth.

Imagine arriving at someone's home. How you are received and where you are received can tell a lot about the trust level that exists between you and the person whose home you are in. Just as in a coaching relationship, the spaces you're invited into can be an indication of the level of connection and authenticity that's been built.

Picture being stuck in the receiving rooms, the more polished spaces of the home where guests are entertained – the rooms with the wooden floors, the tastefully chosen furniture, and the paintings that are hung with precision. As one of The Leadership Academy's long-time coaches used to say,

> When you first get to know someone, you're in the house but you don't get invited into the messy parts; you just remain in the formal living room – you stay in the parts of the house that have been set up for you to see just what your host *wants* you to see.

The real magic of coaching happens beyond those formal spaces. Our colleague elaborated, "You've got to make your way to what I would call the kitchen. The kitchen is where you really get more intimate, where you get to know someone and create." The kitchen, in many homes, is where the authentic, unfiltered experiences happen. It's where meals are prepared, stories are shared, and yes, sometimes it's where we find a big mess, from meals in progress or not yet cleaned up. It is where we break bread. The kitchen signifies vulnerability – a place where we don't have to put on airs. It's the ultimate place of trust.

The challenge is getting access. Many of us, protective and guarded, will find ways to divert guests from seeing our sinks full of dirty dishes. In coaching, the journey from formalities to authenticity requires the coach to **earn** an invite into those deeper, more personal spaces of trust.

▶ SPELL TRUST WITH TWO CS, AN R, AND AN S

Over our nearly two decades of working with coaches, one of the most common mistakes we see people make is thinking that they need to build trust *before* they can truly start coaching. We would argue that the opposite is true – you build trust *by* coaching. Building trust is not magic, and it's not rocket science. When we teach about trust in our leadership development and coach training programs, we break it down to two Cs, an R, and an S: Care, Competence, Reliability, and Sincerity (Feltman, 2008). You can be assured that consciously or unconsciously, your coachee is paying attention to what you say and do aligned to the following questions:

- Care – *Does this person truly care about me – do they have my interests at heart?*
- Competence – *Does time with this person add value – do they help me shift my thinking and my behaviors so that I am more effective in my leadership?*
- Reliability – *Does this person consistently follow through – do they do what they say they will do?*
- Sincerity – *Does this person communicate honestly – do they mean what they say?*

Another trap coaches fall into is to conflate care with empathy and rapport. While empathy and rapport are important to coaching, they do not speak to the depth of what care involves.

To be sure, demonstrating care involves giving your coachee your full attention, showing you understand their feelings and experiences, and providing support. It can even mean making small gestures like bringing a coffee or favorite snack. But it also means being invested enough in your coachee's well-being to offer them feedback to help them grow even when doing so might be uncomfortable for either or both of you.

> "Avoiding discomfort in the coaching relationship prohibits trust from forming. It does not demonstrate care. It means you are not coaching."

HERE ARE SOME EASY WAYS TO START BUILDING A TRUSTING RELATIONSHIP WITH YOUR COACHEE

- Be cognizant of, and create space to attend to, pressing matters for the coachee without sacrificing the focus on leadership development and equity.
- Remember personal interests and relationships; ask follow-up questions (e.g., how was the wedding last weekend?).
- Offer to meet at a local coffee shop or offsite to limit distractions and create an environment conducive to sharing.
- Reliably complete requests for resources from your coachee.
- Follow through on any other commitments that you make, even if they seem small.
- Do not skip the check-in at the beginning and reflection at the end of a coaching conversation.

You can use the following self-reflection questions to unpack how you are building or maintaining trust *each time* you and your coachee meet:

Care	What did showing your coachee that you genuinely care about them look like and sound like in this session?
Competence	What important insight did your coachee walk away with and how do you know? What did you do to facilitate this learning?

(Continued)

Reliability	In what ways did you uphold the overarching agreements that ground your coaching relationship? Did you fully follow through on whatever specific commitments you made previously?
Sincerity	Were there any issues you found yourself sugarcoating or skirting during this session – if so why?

▶ ACKNOWLEDGE WHEN TRUST IS TESTED

It is also important to remember that trust is not static. You can expect there will be times when the trust you have built with a coachee will be tested. For example, when Betty took the helm as principal at her school, she grappled with how to include neurodiverse students on the robotics team, a challenge that preceded her tenure. David, her well-intentioned coach, stepped in with ready advice to navigate this inclusion issue. However, as time passed, Betty withdrew, feeling overwhelmed by David's many suggestions. This led to a crucial conversation where Betty voiced the need for respect for her perspective and expertise.

David thought about what Betty said. He took accountability by revisiting the norms for their interactions and incorporating regular opportunities to exchange feedback into their sessions. David also adjusted his approach to be far less directive and reaffirmed his support for Betty's inclusive vision for her school. They were soon back on track.

Recognizing and understanding your coachee's worldview is foundational to building a meaningful coaching relationship. Our goal as coaches is to foster an environment where leaders feel heard, respected, and empowered to find their own path. When there is a breach of trust, or when we make a mistake, the best thing to do is to acknowledge it directly and take responsibility for efforts to mend the relationship.

▶ MAINTAIN AN INQUIRY STANCE

As a coach, every question you ask is a tool – a catalyst for learning, reflection, and growth. Think of your questions as scaffolding in a well-taught lesson. In the same way, the questions you pose to your coachees can build upon one another, providing the necessary support at each stage of understanding. Mastering the art of asking effective questions that are purposeful and generative means cultivating an inquiry stance and approaching coaching relationships with a sense of curiosity as opposed to positioning yourself as an expert whose role is to advise. Doing so will ensure you are asking authentic questions – ones you don't know the answers to beforehand.

In addition to being authentic, effective questions are purposeful and transparent (Yasharian, 2016). A skilled coach knows what they are trying to achieve through a specific line of questioning. The purpose is clear to both parties, and when there is any doubt, the coach takes time to name the learning purpose and explain why they are interested in learning more. Being transparent in this way demonstrates respect for the coachee and protects against the conversation feeling disingenuous or the coachee feeling manipulated.

Good questions are also usually open-ended. For example, rather than asking, "Did you plan for that to happen?" which can either yield an answer of yes or no, a more effective question could be, "What did you plan to have happen?" Yet while open-ended questions are helpful in this regard, they are no silver bullet. The focus is on constructive dialogue. Effective questions keep the conversation connected to learning and growth and do not generate conversation simply for conversation's sake.

Finally, while debriefing and reflecting are critical to the learning process, leaders will tire quickly of coaching if they are only asked to rethink their past actions and analyze the repercussions. Effective questions that are forward-facing will help your coachee identify implications and consider actions to move forward. For example, "What did you learn about yourself" is more impactful when complemented by, "Why does that matter, and what does it mean for your work?"

Of course, asking great questions is futile if you are not actively listening to your coachee's responses. Be sure to listen intently, not just to the words spoken, but to the emotions conveyed, the body language exhibited, and the subtext that lies beneath the surface. Pay attention to your coachee's framing, their word choices, what they place emphasis on, and what they leave out. As one of The Leadership Academy's coaches put it,

> I say to myself, "take your time and breathe and allow yourself to listen." It's so easy to slip into focusing on asking just the right question. But guess what? If that's where your head space is then you're actually not going to land on the next good question, because the next good question is dependent upon what you hear, what you learn, from your coachee.

Here are common purposes of questions in leadership coaching (Yasharian, 2016):

1. **To build and nurture the relationship between coach and leader.**
   Learning through coaching is powerful when coachees feel that their coach cares about them, shows interest in their lives, and seeks out the details that make them who they are. Examples: Where did your interest in X come from? How's your mentee doing? What did you find most valuable in your principal prep program?
2. **To gain a systemic view of the leader's context.**
   An effective coach is like a detective, trying to learn more about the unique characteristics of the leader's context. They take into account diverse perspectives and how the leader and community make sense of their context. Examples: What is the relationship between the community and the organization like? What patterns can we extrapolate from the student referral data?
3. **To analyze strategy, relationships, and events.**
   This includes exploring causes and antecedents, intended and unintended consequences, priorities, points of leverage, decision-making criteria, data/evidence selection, and thinking critically about the staff's assets, skills, areas for development, and motivations. Effective questions support a leader in taking multiple perspectives and viewing the world with a broader, more expansive mindset. Examples: Why did X go well? What should we do

differently next time? Who was at the table, and who was overlooked or pushed out?
4. **To explore, process, and understand the leader's feelings, thoughts, beliefs, and actions**.
Rich learning can be harvested by reflecting on why leaders feel the way they do, how they respond to something, what motivates them, and how they think about their leadership choices. Effective questions can uncover areas for growth as the coach and leader seek to maximize the coherence across one's thoughts, beliefs, feelings, and actions. Examples: How does that belief or commitment show up in your schedule? When did you notice that you were starting to get bothered? What was happening?
5. **To uncover and raise awareness of a leader's mental models and ways of thinking, being, and seeing the world**.
Not only can questions help a leader better understand *what* they think about something, they can help them understand *how* they think about something. For example: What does that tell you about how you view the role of the assistant principal and your own role? Could there be another way of seeing things, another explanation? Why do you think that is? Is that always true? What assumptions were you making?

▶ GET BELOW THE SURFACE – DIG INTO MEANING-MAKING

As a coach, you are positioned to catalyze transformational leadership, but to do so, you must be able to see the world through your coachee's eyes. You need to delve deep into the layers of individual experiences, core beliefs, motivations, and biases that shape their perspectives. Effective coaching depends on understanding how your coachee perceives and makes meaning of their world, including their core values and the focus they place on specific data and information. This not only helps surface their priorities but also provides you with a window into potential biases. It involves seeing your coachee not just as a leader but also as a complete individual and a learner within their specific context.

> **FOUR BIG QUESTIONS THAT YOU CAN USE TO JUMPSTART YOUR UNDERSTANDING OF HOW YOUR COACHEE THINKS**
>
> - What motivates this person?
> - What's important to them?
> - What do they pay attention to?
> - What are they afraid of?

▶ BRANDON AND AMARI'S STORY

Coach Brandon recalls when, early in their coaching relationship, Amari was a principal opening a brand new small school with just four sixth-grade classes. At the time, Amari was determined to implement a gifted and talented program despite pushback he was getting from his planning team about the resources this would require. He shared with Brandon that he had seen focus group research indicating that parents enrolling students into new schools strongly considered the availability of gifted and talented programs when making their school selections.

Brandon wanted to make sure Amari had really thought through this decision. He asked Amari to share his vision for the program, and then afterward, they talked about whether that vision was unique to the gifted and talented program or something Amari wanted for all his students. Brandon said,

> You will only have four classrooms across the grade – how distinct do you want the gifted class to be from the other three? Given your school's small size, how will this gifted and talented program impact your resources as you open your school?

The more they talked about it, the less clear Amari's rationale for launching the program started to sound. Brandon sensed that Amari was getting frustrated with the conversation and that he was starting to feel defensive. Wanting to be transparent, Brandon said,

> I need you to understand why I am pushing you. Yes, I am concerned about having a sixth-grade gifted class in your inaugural year as a school, but it is your decision, not mine. It's just that I am not sure I understand why you are so invested in launching this right away despite the reservations of your planning team and the implications we have been talking about.

They decided to leave it there and move on to other issues for the remainder of the coaching session. The next time they met, Amari told Brandon that he had done a lot of thinking. He said,

> I realized after our session that I had been holding on to this idea of immediately launching the gifted and talented program because I was in a program like that when I was growing up, and it made a big difference in my life.

Amari sharing this was pivotal and provided Brandon with insight he could use to push Amari's thinking. He started by asking Amari to reflect on all the aspects that made his experience in the gifted and talented program so powerful, and in the following weeks, they focused on what it would take to bring those aspects to life for all of Amari's incoming students. Soon after, the principal decided to hold off on implementing a gifted and talented program, at least for a few years.

This scenario is not meant to serve as a coaching exemplar. Brandon might have avoided causing Amari to grow defensive if he had asked more open-ended questions – perhaps even one as simple as "Why is this so important to you?" Nevertheless, this situation does highlight how learning about Amari's personal educational history helped Brandon understand the values and beliefs underneath the principal's thinking. He was then able to use that information to help Amari align his decisions and actions accordingly.

> **HELPFUL QUESTIONS THAT CAN HELP YOU BEGIN TO GET TO KNOW HOW YOUR COACHEE SEES THEMSELF AND THEIR LEADERSHIP**
>
> - What brought you into the work of education?
> - Of all your accomplishments, what are you most proud of?
> - What values drive you as a person and as a leader?
> - What have you learned about yourself during your leadership journey? In the last year?
> - Considering the road you have traveled in your life and career, which individuals and what experiences had the most profound impact on you as a leader?
> - Who or what inspires you? Why?
> - What are your school's/system's biggest challenges? How do you see your role in attending to these?
> - What do you see as your leadership strengths and vulnerabilities?
> - What are some of your biases? What are some of the things you tend not to notice?

▶ UNCOVER MENTAL MODELS

Asking open-ended questions is one great way of getting to understand your coachee's thinking. Noticing what your coachee pays attention to, what decisions they make, and how they interpret what they see can be even more revelatory. Educators and school leaders are submerged in a sea of data, policies, and interpersonal dynamics. The vast array of information they navigate daily tells a story of their environment, their leadership style, and the challenges they face. What they choose to spotlight amid this overload of information is also telling. Their choices paint a portrait of what they deem essential and, sometimes, what they might inadvertently overlook.

In fact, the narrative your coachee constructs around what they observe offers vital leverage to the coaching process. How an education leader interprets the data they focus on can unmask underlying beliefs, assumptions, and, occasionally, misconceptions and should be leveraged for exploration. For example, hearing a coachee attribute low achievement to factors like family structure can signal a perspective founded on bias-based beliefs.

To be an effective coach, you must understand not only the broader context within which the leader operates but, more importantly, the leader's mental models and their unique way of making sense of themselves and everything around them. Mental models are the assumptions we all carry in our minds, which create a filter for how we see things and lie at the core of the actions we take (Senge, 1990). They can encompass beliefs about the nature of self, other people, organizations, and the larger world. They can be straightforward (e.g., "Hard work leads to success") or complex (e.g., a person's multifaceted belief about leadership).

As coaches, we work through our coachee's mental models to help them understand the impact that those mental models have on their ability to be culturally responsive in their decision-making, actions, and behaviors. We support them in challenging the assumptions that might be limiting their success and in illuminating what might otherwise be obscured or unnoticed. Diving deep into the coachee's interpretative lens is not a courtesy; it's a necessity for several reasons:

- **Self-awareness**: By recognizing their mental models, your coachee can become more aware of the biases they hold that influence how they routinely think and act. This self-awareness can help leaders identify patterns of behavior and thinking that either serve or hinder them in achieving their goals.
- **Change and growth**: To bring about change, sometimes a shift in a person's mental models is necessary. A coach can facilitate this shift by introducing new perspectives and challenging outdated or harmful assumptions.
- **Decision-making**: Recognizing where their perspectives might be limited, a coachee can make more informed choices. Coachees who can see issues from multiple perspectives are better equipped to identify root causes and make decisions that drive effective strategies.

- **Systems-level thinking**: In coaching, our work is about the *self* and the *system*. Leaders cannot shift systems without understanding the beliefs, values, and mental models upon which those systems are built.

Challenging deeply ingrained perceptions is a key piece of systemic change and effective leadership. This process is not a theoretical exercise; it plays out powerfully in the real-world experiences of school leaders.

▶ SOCORRO'S STORY

Socorro still recalls a moment in coaching that forever changed her trajectory as a leader. She had taken on the role of principal at the Oakland high school her mother once attended – a deeply personal undertaking for her. But, she was heartbroken when she discovered in her first year as principal that her students' test scores had dipped. She recounts, "I remember crying all night. I was working so hard, but it didn't show in that one measure of success."

She met with her new coach for a reality check. Socorro poured out her heart about all the efforts she had made. She had drastically reduced behavior referrals, launched campaigns against physical fights, and ensured families felt welcomed on campus. Her coach, listening intently, pointed out a notable omission. "How did academics factor into all this work you just described? You have been working hard, and you have achieved a lot, but I didn't hear you mention anything about ensuring kids had access to grade-level teaching and learning," he said. With a pang of realization, Socorro admitted, "I focused on everything but that." Her coach's words helped her put things into perspective. "Of course, when you have focused so heavily elsewhere, your scores will dip. But this is a marathon, not a sprint. Now as you move forward, you can work on realigning your focus."

Socorro's initial endeavors were not in vain. She had successfully created a safer environment, reduced violence significantly, and earned the trust of the community. But her coach's observations made her realize that, while building a positive culture was essential, she had focused less on the core duty of ensuring access to quality education for all students. The 10 percent of students who were causing disruptions had taken up 90 percent of her attention, distracting her from the bigger picture.

Socorro's initial leadership approach was deeply personal and undoubtedly well-intentioned, focusing on creating a safe and welcoming school environment. However, the journey she undertook with her coach speaks to the complex, and at times uncomfortable, process of re-evaluating the mental maps that guide our leadership priorities. Socorro's assumption was that ensuring a safe and welcoming school environment would naturally lead to academic success, inadvertently causing her to prioritize reducing school violence over directly addressing academic achievement.

When Socorro faced the disheartening news of her students' test scores, it was a stark moment of reckoning. Her coach's probing questions and the subsequent dialogue served as a catalyst for Socorro to confront her existing mental models about school leadership. It was an opportunity to examine whether her actions, while impactful in certain areas, aligned with the comprehensive educational goals she aspired to achieve.

In her coaching sessions, Socorro experienced first-hand the critical coaching principles we have discussed. Self-awareness was sparked as she recognized the oversight in her approach, which emphasized school climate over academic achievement. The need for change and growth became evident as her coach helped her see that her thinking had to expand to include a focus on academics to foster systemic change. This was a decisive step in her decision-making, prompting a shift in strategy as she began to appreciate the balance required to address the holistic challenges of her school.

Socorro's renewed perspective exemplified the substantial impact that examining one's mental models and assumptions can have. By embracing the challenge presented by her coach, she could recalibrate her leadership approach to encompass both a nurturing environment and rigorous academic standards – ultimately aligning her actions with her vision of a school that could meet the needs of all students.

▶ CLIMB DOWN THE LADDER OF INFERENCE

Mental models are what drive people's behaviors, decisions, and actions because they inform what data we notice and how we interpret that data. Coined by organizational psychologist Chris Argyris and familiar to many through Peter Senge's work (Senge, 1990), the "Ladder of Inference" is a conceptual framework that illustrates the mental steps people unconsciously take when absorbing information. Each rung on the ladder represents a step in the process of meaning-making. At the very bottom of the ladder is all the data that is available. When we observe the data, we start unconsciously climbing the ladder, automatically filtering specific details that catch our attention or seem important and attaching meaning to that data based on our own personal interpretations and experiences. Continuing to go up, we instinctively add assumptions, drawing on what we already know, and then use all of this to form conclusions. The conclusions we make shape our beliefs about the world. These beliefs are what drive our actions and, in a reinforcing cycle, influence what data we notice moving forward.

Rungs on the Ladder of Inference
Take Action
From Beliefs
Draw Conclusions
Make Assumptions
Add Meaning
Select Data

We go up the ladder so quickly and so organically that we are typically unaware of how we filter, distort, and generalize information, often excluding certain details as our perceptions are shaped. But by climbing down the Ladder of Inference, leaders can uncover the often-subconscious steps they have taken between observing a piece of data and taking action, including enabling them to identify and challenge the biases and beliefs that may have steered them off course.

One coach shared recently that whenever the Ladder of Inference came up in conversation, he would feel a pang of embarrassment because it would remind him of a first meeting with a new coachee that did not go well. He had been ushered into the principal's office to find two women standing in the room.

> I got in there and saw this very young woman who I took to be in her late twenties and then another woman who seemed more my vintage at the time, maybe close to 50. Well, I walked right over to the older of the two, stuck out my hand, and said, "Nice to meet you! I'm your new coach". She gave me one long look and said, "Oh, I'm not the principal; I'm her secretary. *You just walked right on by the principal.*"

The coach, chagrined to this day, reflected, "The only thing I paid attention to coming into the room was the women's ages. To me, older meant experienced, more knowledgeable, so I assumed the older woman was in a position of authority and, therefore, the principal. It was never a question in my mind; I just went right over to her to introduce myself. I barely even noticed the younger woman."

Staying "low" on the Ladder of Inference means remaining grounded in the raw, observable facts of a situation (the low inference data) and being as objective as possible. You can use questions like the ones that follow to help your coachee see the path of their thinking from those observable facts to their own conclusions and actions.

- What did you actually see or hear? What might you have missed?
- Why do you think you chose to focus on those particular details?
- How did you interpret that? What would be another way to interpret that data?
- What experiences or beliefs might be influencing how you've made meaning of this?
- What are you assuming about the situation or the people involved? What is your evidence?
- What could be a totally different way of looking at this?

You can use the concept of the Ladder of Inference with your coachee to achieve the following:

- **Create self-awareness**: You can introduce the "Ladder of Inference" to raise awareness of how leaders arrive at conclusions without being aware of the assumptions or beliefs that influenced their behavior. It's a tool to illustrate that our actions are often based on beliefs, not just on the facts. It can help a coachee reflect on an emotional reaction and trace it back to a source.
- **Slow down decision-making**: You can encourage a coachee to "climb down the ladder" when making decisions. By revisiting each rung, leaders can understand the data, the interpretations they've made, the assumptions they've used, and how they've arrived at their decisions. This can help a coachee to be deliberate and reflective.
- **Address bias and stereotyping**: The "Ladder" can be used to highlight areas where leaders might be operating under unconscious biases or stereotypes. You can use it to help leaders identify where they might be making generalizations or where their personal beliefs are influencing their interpretations.
- **Deepen reflection**: As part of a leader's development, the ability to reflect on their own actions and decisions is crucial. The "Ladder of Inference" provides a structured way to do this, allowing for deep introspection about how conclusions were reached and actions were decided upon.
- **Promote inquiry over advocacy**: The "Ladder" helps leaders shift from advocating for their views to inquiring about others' views. Instead of stating, "This is what needs to be done," a leader might ask, "Based on what I observed, I came to this conclusion. What did you observe, and what conclusions did you draw?"

▶ TAILOR YOUR APPROACH

As a coach, you have an enormous amount of discretion and are constantly making decisions that shape what and how your coachee is learning when you are together. These discretionary spaces speak to the questions you ask, the feedback you give, and the pacing of your words, the tone you use, and decisions like whether you observe something together or have a discussion in a closed office.

Understanding how your coachee learns allows you to craft effective coaching sessions and make strategic moves to optimize learning and reflection. Here are some strategies to help you be responsive to different learning styles and tendencies.

If	*Then*
They learn by doing	Conversations are not enough. Regularly engage in the work in real time with opportunities to reflect on what is being learned. Co-create assignments or experiments that offer the leader opportunities to practice behaviors or actions in between sessions.
They are a big thinker or a visionary	Create visuals in real time to capture their thinking. Chart ideas on a whiteboard or on paper if in person, or on a digital whiteboard or on a shared screen if virtual. Show them as you go along to ensure you are following their thoughts. Support coachees in considering the details and specifics that implementing their ideas will require.
They have a lot of thoughts at one time	Track their ideas. Put key concepts on a board or in a shared document where you are taking notes as placeholders to come back to. Create a "parking lot" section to put items you both agree to table and return to later.
They promise to have certain conversations but ultimately don't	Practice! Use role play in the moment. Tell your coachee, "Don't just tell me what you will say; say it to me right now as though I am that person."
They seem set in certain opinions, beliefs, or assumptions	Create cognitive dissonance. Take note of the evidence they are using to support the conclusions they draw. Help them gather disconfirming evidence to explore.

(*Continued*)

If	Then
They hesitate to take action and can seem stuck	Work with them to generate micro pilots or experiments that allow them to practice something or test their assumptions but are low risk and will not be of too much consequence if they don't go well.

Finally, understanding how your coachee learns also helps you uncover any assumptions or oversights they may have about how others learn. This awareness has significant implications for their leadership style and effectiveness in building the capacity of their team and staff. By making your own coaching moves visible and talking about why you are using a particular technique, you can enhance your coachee's ability to lead their team more effectively, aiding more students in the long run.

▶ RESPECT BOUNDARIES AND DON'T OVERSHARE

When entering a coaching relationship, your focus is on your coachee's stories and experiences, not your own. While knowing more about you, your experience, and your values can foster deeper trust in the partnership, you also have to be aware of going too far. It is essential to stay within professional limits and ensure that your coachee remains the focal point. Sharing personal anecdotes can offer clarity or show where you are coming from, but beware of diving deep into personal narratives or relying heavily on statements like "In my experience" or "When I was a principal...."

Finding the right balance in sharing is much like walking a tightrope: veer too much one way, and the session becomes about you; drift too far the other, and you might come off as detached. One seasoned coach put it aptly: "In coaching, we navigate the professional, personal, and private spheres. Discerning what best serves the coaching dynamic at any moment is an art." With that in mind, some things that could be very helpful to share with your coachee include:

- Your core values
- Your typical coaching style
- Why do you do this work, and/or why you decided to become a coach

- Key experiences that demonstrate your commitment to accelerating learning for all students through culturally responsive leadership
- How you feel the intersections of your identity inform your approach as a coach

That said, while you can share your experiences as an educator, establish your expertise as a leader in the school system, and even share anecdotes about your work history, be judicious. Consider your purpose in sharing and gauge whether or not your story is germane to your coachee's learning. Remember, the time you are spending with your coachee is not for or about you; rather, you are there to facilitate the leader in advancing their leadership and, ultimately, their students' education.

▶ FINAL THOUGHTS

In this chapter, we explored how you can create the conditions that will allow you to engage in deeper, transformational work with your coachee. We learned that establishing trust is built *through coaching rather than before* coaching. We also explored the leverage that comes with understanding and working from within your coachee's perspectives, enabling them to gain greater self-insight and achieve the growth necessary to address systemic inequities and effect meaningful improvements in the academic success of all students. Lastly, we offered some guidance on how to customize coaching sessions and maintain boundaries to maximize your coachee's learning.

BACK TO YOU

- How do you currently demonstrate care, competence, reliability, and sincerity in your coaching relationships? *Pick one new way to demonstrate one of these and use it in your next coaching session.*
- How have your own mental models, assumptions, or biases come into play in your coaching? *Practice trying to stay low on the Ladder of Inference.*
- What have you noticed about your coachee's learning style? *Identify the learning style of your coachee and make one shift in your next coaching session to optimize their learning.*

Bibliography

Argyris, C. (1990). *Overcoming organizational defenses: Facilitating organizational learning.* Allyn & Bacon.

Feltman, C. (2008). *The thin book of trust; an essential primer for building trust at work.* Thin Book Publishing.

Senge, Peter M. (1990). *The fifth discipline: The art and practice of the learning organization.* Doubleday/Currency.

Yasharian, F. (2016). *Effective Questioning for Leadership Development.* The Leadership Academy.

Bringing Your Coachee to the Learning Edge

> *I think a big part of it is just to always make sure that there is a push. Somewhere during the coaching conversation, there needs to be something that pushes their thinking farther than where they were. I'm always intentional about that.*
>
> – Coach, The Leadership Academy

BIG IDEAS IN THIS CHAPTER

- Discomfort is an inherent part of learning and something to intentionally provoke and contain as part of the coaching process.
- Feedback that isolates behavior and its impact is a powerful tool for supporting self-insight.
- Leverage for long-lasting change comes from deeper levels of dialogue that help coachees see how they are implicated in a situation or challenge.
- The iceberg construct can help coachees use systems thinking to uncover the root causes of organizational challenges and inequities.

In Chapter 4, we shared concepts and strategies to create the conditions for deeper learning. You read about how to build trust through coaching, the importance of understanding your coachee's context and mental models, and techniques

DOI: 10.4324/9781003010876-6

to tailor your coaching sessions. As we have been discussing, to truly confront systemic inequities and transform conditions for students, your coachee must not only be willing to examine their own beliefs about children, learning, and school, but also practice new thinking and behaviors and be able to support other adults in doing so as well. As a coach, finding the right balance of support and challenge will help you bring your coachee to this learning edge and maintain it over time.

▶ BALANCE SUPPORT AND CHALLENGE

The *Equity Leadership Dispositions* we outlined in Chapter 2 don't just describe the foundational aspects of culturally responsive leadership; they highlight how the *self* and the *system* are interconnected when it comes to leading change. There is no getting around it: the hard work of transforming schools and school systems requires reflection, experimentation, and practice on a personal and organizational level. To coach someone effectively in this context requires creating a **holding environment**, a space that is safe and supportive enough for your coachee to be vulnerable while also generating enough pressure to keep them sufficiently motivated to wrestle with the demands of dismantling deeply seated inequities. The power of the holding environment lies in its ability to nudge individuals beyond their existing paradigms, helping them gravitate toward broader and more profound understandings of themselves and their surroundings (Kegan, 1994). Some practitioners liken the idea of a holding environment to a pressure cooker. For it to function properly, you need to apply enough heat to the device while also ensuring sufficient steam can escape (Heifetz et al., 2009).

The interplay between the holding environment's dynamics of high support and high challenge is vital to coaching because growth and learning occur in the **productive zone of disequilibrium** (PZD). This concept, as coined by Heifetz et al. (2009), highlights the optimal range of distress that motivates adaptive work, providing just enough stress to stimulate change without overwhelming or paralyzing individuals. Your job as a coach is to offer the right balance of support, celebration, and challenge that will keep your coachee in this productive zone, propelling them toward growth and action while helping them sustain the resilience and energy they need.

But provoking discomfort in the service of learning can be a difficult practice for coaches to adopt. One coach, a former superintendent from the Midwest, reflected on how she came to embrace the notion of challenging her coachees:

> As a coach, I've had to unlearn a lot of things. While I used to focus on building a 'good relationship' with coachees, I now focus more on whether or not my coaching is helping to advance their thinking. It's essential to consider who is doing the heavy lifting in this process. Are we, as coaches, pushing our coachees to their full potential? I've discovered that guiding them to a place of slight discomfort, a space that challenges both of us, is where the most significant learning occurs. This approach has reshaped my coaching philosophy, emphasizing growth over comfort.

The following are some strategies you can use to both challenge and support your coachee (Yasharian, 2016).

Challenge your Coachee

- **Linger on the topic you are exploring before moving toward a solution**.
  Fight your urge to move quickly toward a solution so you can mine the experience for more learning. Heifetz et al. (2009) argues that for real learning to happen, people must situate themselves in both the problem and solution. Use your questions to explore the topic, problem, or experience rather than the solution, and lean into the discomfort. For example, instead of immediately asking, "How will you fix this?," explore, "Why did this happen? What role did race or power play in this situation? What are the consequences?"

- **Create cognitive dissonance.**
  Cognitive dissonance is a psychological phenomenon that occurs when a person holds two or more contradictory beliefs or values, or when their behavior does not align with their beliefs or values. For example, a leader who values collaboration and participative decision-making but tends to make unilateral decisions may experience this tension. Share data and offer feedback to help your coachee see potential disconnects. The purpose is not to catch your coachee in a "gotcha" moment but rather to prompt introspection.
- **Use silence.**
  After asking an effective question, sharing a low-inference observation, or delivering purposeful feedback, take a breath and pause. Look at your coachee, remain silent, and count to seven in your head. While it may feel awkward to maintain silence, let your coachee be the first one to talk. Doing so keeps the spotlight on the issue at hand, puts the pressure on your coachee, and transfers the "thinking work" of coaching to its rightful owner – the coachee!
- **Encourage more than "I don't know."**
  It doesn't matter how effectively you frame a question if your coachee's only response is "I don't know." Let your coachee know that you won't accept that response, and ask them to think more deeply. For example, "I know it's hard to think about how your actions contributed to the problem, and nothing comes immediately to mind, but let's take a moment and think about it. How do you think someone else could have interpreted your actions?"
- **Focus on the hard stuff.**
  Keep the attention on the nature of the adaptive challenge your coachee is facing and the gap between where the coachee is and where they want to be. Stick to purpose and be relentless in keeping to that purpose across sessions. For example, ask questions such as, "What are you doing to shift the hearts and minds of the resistors? How will you follow up on what you did two weeks ago?

How are you modeling the vulnerability you expect from your grade-level leaders?"

Coaching brings leaders to the point of discomfort so that they can ultimately come out more confident, capable, and conscious of their capacity to make change effectively. But maintaining the holding environment is not just about provoking discomfort, it is also about containing it so the work does not become too overwhelming or frustrating. Learning journey, and as they advance in their learning, celebrate their achievements and provide the support they need to stay energized and resilient.

Support your Coacheee

- **Recognize past success.**
  Discuss strategies your coachee has used to successfully overcome past challenges. Remind your coachee of their talents, flexibility, and ability to apply learning to novel situations. Have your coachee articulate the specific steps they took. Example, "How did you work with your third-grade team to ensure they were able to meet all of their students' needs? What specifically did you do? What does that experience tell you about yourself? Your ability to move instruction? Your ability to handle this (new) situation?"
- **Be transparent.**
  Name the fact that you are intentionally creating discomfort for your coachees in the name of learning. Seeing your questions, observations, and feedback as strategic moves rather than hostile provocation can lower the pressure. Consequently, this approach can empower your coachee to turnkey this strategy when interacting with others. Example: "I believe challenging situations can be great opportunities for learning, so I'm intentionally sticking with this topic and putting on the pressure. If we sit in this place of discomfort for a little while longer, we may land on some important insights or ideas."

- **Invite the coachee to consider a way forward.**
  After exploring a topic sufficiently, invite the coachee to consider how the organization can move forward. Explore their team's role and the personal actions they can take. Have your coachee name the work that lies ahead and identify the difficult conversations that need to happen. Encourage them to consider what small, medium, and big steps they can take to advance their goal and what progress might feel like. Example: "So what conversations do you need to have? What will your goal be in those conversations? What will be hard about that? What feelings will come up for you?"
- **Create opportunities to practice.**
  As you help your coachee develop new habits, skills, and ways of being and thinking, it can be helpful to use your coaching session as a place to practice. Consider engaging your coachee in role-play, having them script-out a message they want to deliver, or doing other preparation for a critical action step with you by their side. Your coachee can try something new with you before "taking it live" with other constituents. Example: "Let's take time now to organize what your PTA message needs to include." "Let's role-play how that teacher conference will go – I'll be the teacher." "Can we chart out what the new structure will look like and what your and other people's responsibilities will be?"
- **Celebrate.**
  Celebrate the courage your coachee demonstrated in engaging in a difficult conversation, the risk your coachee took at the last faculty meeting, and the small but deliberate change in their own behavior that they've been working on. Collect low-inference data and help your coachee notice the positive consequences of your work together and the resultant incremental changes in classrooms and hallways. Lastly, take time to spotlight any positive feedback you or your coachee receive about your coachee's leadership. Don't let positivity be drowned out by the noise of constant criticism as your coachee takes on an entrenched problem.

▶ BE GENEROUS WITH THE GIFT OF FEEDBACK

Feedback is an integral part of coaching and offers a direct pathway to both celebrating and challenging your coachee. As one seasoned coach shared recently, "I've noticed that many leaders are their own harshest critics, so I try to shine a light on their triumphs, emphasizing the brilliance of their journey." Whether sharing warm or cool feedback, coaches are most effective when they:

- Frame feedback to optimize impact, taking into account the leader's context, learning preferences, and timing to ensure benefit.
- Provide feedback that is based on low-inference data and observation, and is timely, applicable, useful, honest, and purposeful.
- Remain cognizant of emotional tenor, eye contact, body language, and the impact of their words.

It is vitally important to consider how aspects of identity and power are at play in the exchange of feedback. Your experiences, biases, beliefs, and perspectives color how you give and receive feedback, just as aspects of your coachee's identity inform how they interpret and internalize what you say. For instance, cultural norms and past experiences might make one coachee more receptive to direct feedback, while another might find it confrontational. At times, a female leader might feel her feedback is received differently than her male counterpart's, and a person of color might wrestle with feedback that feels tinted with bias, however unintentional. You, as a coach, are not exempt from these influences either. Your own unconscious biases, formed by a lifetime of experiences and societal influences, can unwittingly shape what and how you choose to share. For example, are you unintentionally softer on feedback with someone of a different gender, race, or background, fearing that you would come off too harshly? Or, inversely, are you inadvertently more critical, driven by the desire to ensure they meet a certain standard?

The path to effective coaching is paved with self-awareness. It requires an ongoing commitment to examining biases, acknowledging limitations in your perspective, and ensuring they don't cloud your judgment or interactions. Only by understanding and acknowledging these dynamics can you create a coaching environment that's truly equitable, fostering growth and trust for both you and your coachee.

▶ SITUATION-BEHAVIOR-IMPACT (SBI) FEEDBACK STRUCTURE

While there are a host of effective techniques for sharing feedback, one approach we find particularly useful in fostering self-awareness and helping coachees see the impact of their behaviors is the Situation-Behavior-Impact (SBI)™ structure developed by the Center for Creative Leadership (CCL, 2022; Weitzel, 2000a). SBI helps make feedback straightforward, objective, and inescapable. With SBI, you can achieve the following:

- Capture the **Situation**: Detail the specific occasion or event.
- Describe the **Behavior**: Relate the observed actions, avoiding judgments by using low-inference data.
- Specify the **Impact**: Communicate the results of the observed behavior.

The SBI structure is based on three simple sentence stems that serve to ensure the feedback you are providing remains concise and to the point.

Situation	Behavior	Impact
When you…	You…	As a result…

▶ FRANCISCO AND JOHN'S STORY

John was the principal of a middle school with an increasingly diverse student population. Francisco, his coach, was engaged by the district office to support John in navigating the challenges of returning to in-person schooling following the pandemic. During one of their check-ins, when Francisco asked how John was doing, the principal replied,

> I'm hanging in there, but we are still seeing lots of fallout from COVID. A lot of the grades are down. Just today, one of the parents, Ms. Gonzalez, called me very upset about her daughter Marisol. She said Marisol usually gets Bs on her report card, but this year, all her grades are down, and she even got a D in math from Mr. Reynolds.

Mr. Reynolds, Francisco already knew, had over a decade of teaching experience and was someone John admired for his lesson plans and orderly classroom. John continued,

> I met with Mr. Reynolds. He told me Marisol hasn't been submitting her homework on time, and homework is 15% of her grade. On top of that, Mr. Reynolds said that Marisol seems distracted during class, and class participation is another 15%. Now, I know Marisol – she's a great kid, and I feel for her, I really do. Ms. Gonzalez is a nurse, so she's out of the house all day, which leaves Marisol in charge of her younger brother. I don't think the dad is in the picture much. The kid really doesn't have the support at home that she needs – especially now. It's not just Marisol, though. I think Mr. Reynolds and every other teacher has a handful of kids in their classes whose home lives right now are making it impossible for them to be successful.

When the principal stopped speaking, Francisco paused for a moment to consider his next coaching move.

> "John," he began, "I heard you say two things that I would like to unpack. The first is your assumption that Marisol's dad is not involved and that she doesn't have support at home. The second is that when you were describing the situation of many students in your school, you said, 'Their home lives are making it impossible for them to be successful.' I wonder how your beliefs about the Gonzalez family dynamics are informing your expectations of Marisol as a student. Let's start by unpacking why you are assuming the dad isn't in the picture."

In coaching, feedback is not an end unto itself but should be used to open the door for reflection and exploration regarding the implications of what has occurred. We think of these as the 'So What?' 'Now What?' questions. Here are a couple of examples of how Francisco could have used the SBI feedback structure, along with additional follow-up questions to explore further with John.

1. ***When you*** were describing the situation of many students at your school, ***you*** said, "their home lives were making it 'impossible' for them to succeed." ***As a result***, you absolved yourself and the other teachers of the responsibility to create the conditions for them to succeed. *What do you see as your role in creating the conditions students need to be successful?*
2. ***When you*** shared about the grading policy, ***you*** explained that at least 30% of Marisol's grade is informed by things other than her mastery of the skills and content. ***As a result***, you communicated that Marisol is getting a D whether or not she knows the math. *What factored into your decision-making on this policy? Are there any adjustments you might consider?*

Remember that feedback in coaching is reciprocal and a critical part of establishing a trust-based, authentic relationship. Be sure to ask your coachee for feedback regularly and hold yourself accountable for giving your coachee the feedback they need to grow. If you do find yourself hesitating to share feedback, you may be attempting to shield yourself or your coachee from discomfort at the expense of their learning. A good practice is to reflect after each coaching session and ask yourself, "What feedback, if any, did I withhold from sharing and why?"

▶ SYLVIA AND PAULA'S STORY

Sylvia, the principal of a bustling middle school, sat across from Paula, her seasoned coach, for their regular check-in. Sylvia had always been an open book with Paula, and today's conversation was no exception. They began with pleasantries, but it wasn't long before Sylvia's concerns spilled out. Sylvia had taken a hard look at how the English language arts and math teachers were supporting neurodiverse students in their classrooms. She had initiated conversations with the teachers, emphasizing the importance of preparing all students for high school and not sidelining anyone during the precious hours they had for learning. Sylvia had hoped her words would resonate, but the responses from the teachers left her disheartened. They agreed in principle, but in the same breath, they insisted that the inclusive practices weren't working for "those" kids.

Paula listened intently, her gaze never wavering from Sylvia. "Do they know how to include the students effectively?" Paula asked, her voice steady. Sylvia hesitated, her fingers tracing the edge of her coffee cup. "I don't think so," she admitted. "It seems they're waiting for the special ed teacher to figure it out." In addressing her teachers' reluctance to adapt their methods, Sylvia had advised them to consult with the special ed teacher and to use the data from the Individualized Education Programs (IEPs) to differentiate instruction. Her voice now got quieter. "I get that it's hard, though," she confessed to Paula, admitting, finally, that she had never led an inclusion class herself, and the path forward was shrouded in fog.

Paula's question sliced through the uncertainty. "Where can you go for support?" Sylvia shared that the district had a specialist, an instructional coach, but she hadn't reached out. "What's preventing you from reaching out now?" Paula pressed further. The answer, when it came, was a mixture of pride and uncertainty. As the principal, Sylvia felt pressure to project a certain persona, one of unwavering competence, especially since she had prior experience in schools with high numbers of IEPs. The expectation, it seemed, was that she already had all the answers. Paula watched the struggle play across Sylvia's face, the internal battle between asking for help and maintaining her carefully curated image. It was a moment of vulnerability, a critical juncture in Sylvia's leadership journey. Sylvia had thought she could handle it, but the reality was different. She was adept at many aspects of her job, but this was a gap in her expertise – one that she could no longer ignore.

The coaching session ended with Sylvia's resolving to make the call to bring in the district's specialist, to shelve the facade of complete expertise, and to address the needs of her teachers – and ultimately, the students. It was a decisive moment facilitated by Paula's probing. Paula had kept pressing on the "whys" behind the stagnation and nudging Sylvia just enough to see beyond her self-imposed barriers. Instead of adhering rigidly to an image of all-knowing leadership, Sylvia gingerly resolved to take a more collaborative and learning-focused approach. This change would not only benefit her personal growth as a principal but also ripple through her school, fostering a more inclusive and effective educational environment.

▶ ATTEND TO THE TECHNICAL BUT EMBRACE THE ADAPTIVE

Coaching that succeeds in generating new thinking on the part of an education leader but falls short of yielding any corresponding behavior will make little difference to the students that leader serves. Culturally responsive leadership means confronting biases (one's own and others'), facilitating learning, dismantling the structures that perpetuate student marginalization, and ultimately shifting instruction and culture through new ways of being and doing so that all students can thrive. The challenges involved are adaptive in that they are multilayered and complex, beyond the scope of quick fixes or simple solutions. In Sylvia's case, for example, the real problem wasn't the lack of available support from the district or even a dearth of known strategies for team teaching neurodiverse students. The sticking point had been an adaptive one, rooted in Sylvia's self-image and commitment to being perceived as an expert by her staff and her colleagues in the district.

Ronald Heifetz, Alexander Grashow, and Marty Linsky (2009) describe the difference between adaptive challenges and technical problems this way:

> While technical problems may be very complex and critically important…, they have known solutions that can be implemented by current know-how. They can be resolved

through the application of authoritative expertise and through the organization's current structures, procedures, and ways of doing things. Adaptive challenges can only be addressed through changes in people's priorities, beliefs, habits, and loyalties. Making progress requires going beyond any authoritative expertise to mobilize discovery, shedding certain entrenched ways, tolerating losses, and generating the new capacity to thrive anew.

(p. 19)

Technical Problems	Adaptive Challenges
• Solved with known solutions • Addressed with current structures and processes • Need applied authority or expertise • "Information"	• Resolved by discovery, trial, and error • Require new ways of doing and being • Involve changes in mindset and priorities • "Transformation"

As an FCB Coach, you can and should support your coachees in addressing or accessing assistance for technical problems when needed, but their growth will come from the time you spend grappling with the adaptive challenges. Keep in mind that while adaptive issues require a facilitative approach, technical problems are a different story. An easy acronym we at The Leadership Academy have found to help us remember when a more instructive or directive approach would be best is what we refer to as - B.O.N.U.S.

- **Basic**: If basic information is needed, provide it. There is no reason to delay sharing the nuts and bolts of the role or responses to technical challenges leaders are facing that you can help resolve quickly.
- **Overwhelmed**: If your coachee is overwhelmed, a facilitative approach may not be helpful in the moment. Give them enough guidance so they can move forward.
- **New or nonnegotiable**: If your coachee needs information or help with something they haven't encountered

before, offer it. In the same vein, if your coachee is dealing with a system-level directive or compliance issue that is nonnegotiable, support them in getting it done.
- **Urgent**: If your coachee is facing an urgent challenge, there is no time to be facilitative. Provide the support they need in the immediate to navigate the issue. You can revisit and debrief for learning later on.
- **Safety and stagnation**: Don't delay on anything regarding safety – tell your coachee what to do. In addition, if your ongoing attempts to facilitate your coachee's learning are not yielding results, offer more direction to help get them unstuck.

In his book, *Coaching the Team at Work*, David Clutterbuck (2007) offers a helpful construct for understanding the various levels of dialogue that coaching requires. Each level is necessary for the ability to achieve adaptive change increasing with the depth of the dialogue. An inflection point exists as discussions move from the level of strategy, which is externally focused, to dialogue for self-insight through which the leader acknowledges their own role in the situation at hand. The most impact is to be had through dialogue for behavioral change as coachees translate their awareness into new ways of engaging with the system and world around them. Clutterbuck's levels of dialogue are:

- **Social dialogue**: Builds and maintains the rapport and trust that underpins effective learning relationships.
- **Technical dialogue**: Helps the coachee understand the systems and processes essential to doing a task.
- **Tactical dialogue**: Helps the coachee work out practical ways to deal with presenting problems or issues they face in their context.
- **Strategic dialogue**: Takes the process deeper, providing an opportunity to examine the context and big picture behind an issue and to develop longer-term solutions.
- **Dialogue for self-insight**: Changes the focus of conversation from the external environment to the internal. For example, it examines how the coachee is contributing to

the problems they experience; It helps work out what they really want from a set of difficult circumstances and encourages self-belief.
- **Dialogue for behavioral change**: Builds on these insights and applies them to support the adoption of new behaviors and actions.

It is important to note that not every level of dialogue is called for in every coaching session, and coaches need not approach the levels consecutively. However, we would agree with Clutterbuck that, in our experience, the levels of dialogue become increasingly challenging for coaches the deeper they go. To avoid the discomfort of dealing directly with matters of personal leadership, coaches sometimes shy away from engaging their coachees in conversations that would foster self-insight and behavioral change. Instead, they remain planted in tactical or strategic conversations that, while useful, do not fully support the exploration that adaptive challenges demand. This is why the SBI framework we described earlier can be particularly helpful in encouraging dialogue for self-insight: it offers a simple, yet powerful, way to zero in specifically on someone's behavior and its impact.

Clutterbuck's framework can help you consider the types of questions that will best serve your coachee at any given time and are aligned with a learning purpose. Here are a few examples of questions, adapted from Clutterbuck (2007), that may be helpful to better understand the nuances that exist among the levels. In Appendix C, you can find more sample questions at each level of dialogue.

Social	How is it going?
	What is top of mind for you?
	What are you looking forward to this week, month, etc.?
	How are you taking care of yourself?
Technical	When are the deadlines for submitting?
	Where can you access the information you need?
	What do the district's regulations say about that?
	How has the school approached this in the past?

(Continued)

Tactical	Who will you involve? When will the team first meet? Why is this so important at this time? How will you respond?
Strategic	What will success look like, and how will you measure it? What might be the unintended consequences of taking this approach? What capacity will you need to build on the part of the department now to get the results you seek later? How will you motivate your team to engage?
Self-Insight	What assumptions are you making about this? How have you contributed to this issue? What's been your role in perpetuating the situation? What feels hard for you in this case? What does this pattern tell you about what you are prioritizing?
Behavioral Change	How will you ensure your values show up in the decisions you are making? What would it look like for you to test that assumption? What is one shift you want to practice next time you engage with them? How will your new routine support you in holding them accountable?

Recall Francisco and John's story from earlier. Their story helps illustrate the myriad choice points coaches make as they align their coaching moves to learning purpose. Francisco might have taken a tactical approach, supporting the principal in responding to Ms. Gonzalez and coming up with a specific plan for Marisol. Or he could have focused on strategy by engaging the principal in developing a plan to dig deeper into the data and address the pattern of lower grades among the student body. Instead, Francisco chose to leverage John's own words as an opportunity to foster greater awareness (self-insight) of the assumptions he was making.

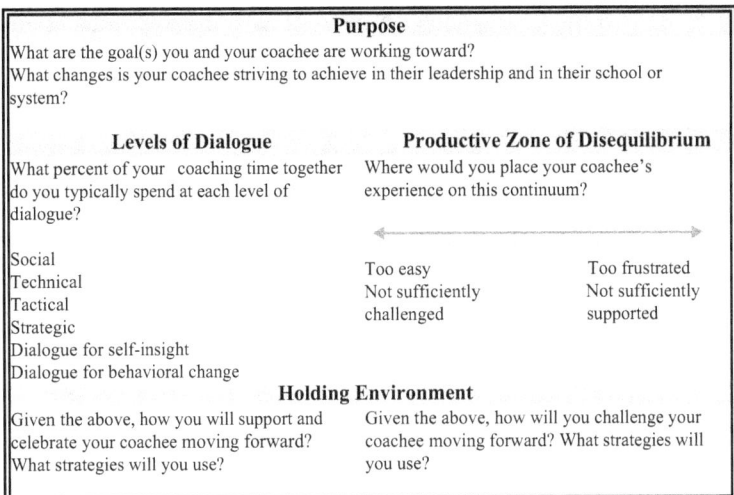

Figure 5.1 Strengthening the Holding Environment Graphic Organizer

What do you see are the advantages and limitations of each approach? At what level of dialogue would you center the conversation if you were John's coach?

▶ DIVE DEEP INTO ICY WATERS

> **"**You can use this graphic organizer (Figure 5.1) to reflect on the balance of support and challenge you are striking in your coaching and to consider what adjustments you might make to maximize learning and impact with your coachee.**"**

Just as Clutterbuck's levels of dialogue point to paradigm and behavioral shifts as the bedrock for adaptive work, creating sustainable and lasting change in schools is predicated on a leader's awareness of – and ability to intervene in – the beliefs and corresponding structures that uphold inequities. The **iceberg construct** is a systems thinking model (Senge, 1990) that can help leaders delve into the root causes of complex organizational challenges and surface the entrenched relationships, interdependencies, and mindsets that perpetuate harm.

The thing to remember about icebergs is that as gargantuan as they may seem from the surface, most of their mass lies submerged in the frigid depths of the ocean. It is only the tip that we see jutting above the water. To use the iceberg as a construct for systemic transformation, imagine that tip as an event that happens or a problem that arises. While we may perceive it as a singular instance, it is likely connected to deeper patterns lying beneath the surface that may not be visible to us without looking below the waterline. In fact, if we go even deeper than those patterns, we will find the structures that give rise to them, and, finally, if we go all the way to the bottom of the iceberg, we will find the beliefs and mental models upon which those structures were built. The further down you go, the harder things are to shift but the more leverage you have to make real and lasting change.

Event
Patterns
Structures
Beliefs/Mental Models

We can look again at Francisco and John's story using the iceberg. Ms. Gonzalez's call about Marisol's D in math was the event. However, if John reacted to the call solely as an isolated incident, he would be doing little to address the conditions that led to its occurrence.

Looking more closely, Marisol's D in math is part of a number of related patterns detectable in the story: The school is increasingly diverse, there is "fall out" from COVID, lots of grades are down, and per the principal, there are students in every class who, like Marisol, are not succeeding. A root cause analysis would surely surface a variety of structures and processes underlying those patterns. For example, one structure at play is the grading policy. Mr. Reynolds, for example, allows for at least 30% of students' grades in math to be based on behaviors like speaking up in class or handing in homework instead of their mastery of the skills and content. This speaks to mental models and beliefs in the school about learning, engagement, grades, and assessment. And, as Francisco noted in his conversation with John, there are likely additional assumptions and biases at play that the school staff will need to reckon with connected to students' identities, family structures, and socio-economic backgrounds.

As a coach, you can help the leaders you support effect long-lasting improvements in the student and classroom experience by building their capacity to look below the water line to uncover patterns of inequity, trends, and

recurring challenges that persist over time. As they dive deeper, they will find the structures that hold those patterns in place and ultimately the deeply ingrained beliefs, values, and assumptions – the mental models – that shape the system's overall behavior. In Appendix E, you will find a school-level diagnostic tool based on the iceberg that you can use with school leaders and teams to unpack key areas of school practice and explore root causes.

▶ FINAL THOUGHTS

In this chapter, we explored how to create a holding environment and provide a balance of support and challenge to maximize learning and bring the coachee to their learning edge. We learned that the most effective coaches focus on developing adaptive leadership, while also providing technical support when needed. To that end, we examined the importance of helping coachees understand their own thinking, reckon with the impact of their behaviors, and practice new approaches. We also introduced how the iceberg construct can be used to identify leverage for transforming systems and classroom experiences in service of improving outcomes for all students.

BACK TO YOU

- Where would you place your coachee in the productive zone of disequilibrium? *Try one new strategy for support or challenge to maximize learning.*
- In what ways do identity and power play into your feedback conversations with your coachee? *Have a conversation with your coachee on how they like to receive feedback.*
- At what levels of dialogue do most of your coaching conversations currently take place? At which levels do you spend the least amount of time? Why? *In your next coaching session, try using some of the question prompts in this chapter and in the tool in Appendix C to move the conversation to the levels of self-insight and behavioral change.*
- How can you use the iceberg construct to help your coachee understand where they have leverage to make a change in their own school or system? *Try out the school-level diagnostic tool Appendix E with your coachee.*

Bibliography

Center for Creative Leadership (CCL). Use situation-behavior-impact (SBI)™ to understand intent. November 18, 2022. https://www.ccl.org/articles/leading-effectively-articles/closing-the-gap-between-intent-vs-impact-sbii/

Clutterbuck, David. (2007). *Coaching the team at work.* Nicholas Brealey Publishing.

Cohen, Geoffrey, Steele, Claude, & Ross, Lee. (1999). The mentor's dilemma: Providing critical feedback across the racial divide. *Society for Personality and Social Psychology, 35*(10), 1302–1318.

Heifetz, Ronald A., Linsky, Marty, & Grashow, Alexander. (2009). *The practice of adaptive leadership: Tools and tactics for changing your organization and the world.* Harvard Business Review Press.

Hoppe, Michael. (2007). Lending an ear: Why leaders must learn to listen actively. *Leadership in Action, 27*(4), 11–14.

Kegan, R., & Lahey, L. (2016). *An everyone culture: Becoming a deliberately developmental organization.* Harvard Business Review Press.

Kegan, Robert. (1994). *In over our heads: The mental demands of modern life.* Harvard University Press.

Kim, D. (1999). *Introduction to systems thinking.* Pegasus Communications.

Kumar-Lanka, Vijaya. Coaching agile teams through cognitive dissonance. *LinkedIn Blog.* September 20, 2018. https://www.linkedin.com/pulse/coaching-agile-teams-through-cognitive-dissonance-vijaya-kumar-lanka/

Meadows, D. M. (1999). *Leverage points: Places to intervene in a system.* Sustainability Institute.

Senge, P. M. (1990). *The fifth discipline: The art and practice of the learning organization,* 1st ed. Doubleday/Currency.

Texas Education Agency. (2023). *Texas gateway: Phase 3 – teach & observe.* https://www.texasgateway.org/resource/phase-3-teach-and-observe

Weitzel, Sloan R. (2000a). *Feedback that works: How to build and deliver your message.* Center for Creative Leadership.

Weitzel, Sloan R. (2000b). Three keys to effective feedback. *Leadership in Action, 20*(3), 8–11.

Yasharian, F. (2016). *Effective questioning for leadership development.* The Leadership Academy.

Chapter 6

Maximizing Impact in Practical Ways

"I don't leave a session without asking two important questions. The first is, "What are the next steps? Give me two to three next steps that you want to work on from now until the next time we meet." The second question is, "What did you find valuable in this session?"

— Coach, The Leadership Academy

BIG IDEAS IN THIS CHAPTER

- Each coaching relationship generally has four phases. Using a wide-angle lens to see the full arc of the coaching engagement from initiation to closure helps you to strategically plan for each session.
- The $(CPR)^2$ structure can help you plan individual coaching sessions for success.
- By getting closer to the action and working side by side with your coachee, you can have a great impact on student learning.
- To ensure the learning and impact are long-lasting and extend beyond your coaching engagement, it is important to mindfully plan for closure.

The adaptive work necessary to foster culturally responsive leadership requires coaches to nimbly toggle between the "balcony and dance floor" (Heifetz & Linsky, 2002). As the coach, you need to be fully present and on the "dance floor" with your coachee, shadowing them during classroom walkthroughs, helping them prepare for meetings with parents, or observing them lead continuous improvement cycles based on formative assessments. But you also need to be able to step back and away from all the action and view the whole "dance floor" from a greater distance, or the "balcony". Going from the micro to the macro affords you as complete a picture as possible of what is happening so you can strategically plan for and adjust the course of action.

▶ USE A WIDE-ANGLE LENS

While coaching work itself tends to be iterative, it can be helpful to conceptualize the sequential aspects involved. A wide-angle perspective puts the entirety of the coaching engagement into focus so you can understand its various phases from inception to completion (Figure 6.1).

While this depiction provides some explicit and discrete components, it is not intended to represent rigid guidelines that always need to be adhered to in a step-by-step manner. Every coaching engagement is unique and progresses at its own pace. You and your coachee might even experience being in multiple phases simultaneously as your relationship develops and the goals are sharpened.

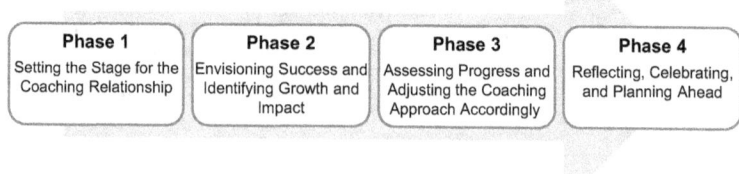

Figure 6.1 The Leadership Academy's Coaching Road Map

©The Leadership Academy

Phase 1: Setting the Stage for the Coaching Relationship

In this phase, the coaching engagement is initiated and you and your coachee begin. As mentioned in Chapter 3, the five key steps to setting a strong foundation include:

1. Establish a Shared Understanding of the Purpose of FCB Coaching
2. Set Agreements to Maximize Learning and Development
3. Agree Upon Basic Logistics
4. Determine Goals for Impact
5. Address Disengagement Directly

Your first few sessions with your coachee are important opportunities to get to know them and begin building trust. Work together to decide on some initial activities like classroom visits or a learning walk that will allow you to see your coachee in action and learn more about their context. At the same time, be sure to surface their immediate needs and provide resources or technical assistance if needed.

Phase 2: Envisioning Success and Identifying Growth and Impact

The second phase of a coaching engagement includes ongoing relationship building and the honing of goals as you and your coachee identify the leadership growth areas necessary to achieve the system or school-level objectives. While you continue to lay the groundwork for the coaching and drive the work, you and your coachee share ownership as you co-develop a vision for success. Refer to Chapter 3 for recommended strategies and Appendix B for a workbook you can utilize with your coachee. As coach, your priorities in this phase are to:

- Continue cultivating trust and strengthening your coaching relationship.
- Refine the goal-setting process, ensuring leadership development is informed by and aligned to the strategic objectives of the school and system, connected to a leader-facing

framework, and focused on improving instructional practices.
- Facilitate the envisioning of what goal attainment entails and identify the mindsets and behaviors that could contribute to or hinder advancement.
- Co-create an initial approach to periodically gather evidence and assess progress and impact.
- Co-develop a plan for you to observe the leader in action and provide feedback to promote self-reflection and behavioral change on the part of the coachee.

Phase 3: Assessing Progress and Adjusting the Coaching Approach Accordingly

As coaching continues, the third phase of an engagement contains a pivotal inflection point – the midpoint check-in. The intended outcome at this juncture is for your coachee to emerge from the conversation prepared to (1) articulate a realistic "desired state" of where they want the school or system to be at the end of the coaching engagement and (2) identify a set of priorities around which to focus their efforts to achieve that desired state. These then serve to inform any adjustments necessary to the coaching approach so that leaders can forge ahead in stewarding the work of their schools or systems. To ensure a productive and fruitful midpoint check-in, both you and your coachee need to collaboratively:

- Assess progress toward coaching goals by collecting and examining evidence of leadership growth and impact. Discuss what changes your coachee expects to see as a result of their efforts and where these changes can be seen.
- Evaluate the current effectiveness of the coaching relationship and recalibrate, identifying what tweaks or adjustments might be needed over the remainder of the coaching engagement.

The following is a tool to support preparing for and engaging in a midpoint check-in conversation.

MIDPOINT CHECK-IN PLANNER

Part 1: Prework Reflection Questions for You, the Coach

- How will you frame the purpose of this conversation?
- Where might you push your coachee's thinking ahead of time? What do they need to reflect on before you meet?
- What are you and your coachee looking at to inform this conversation?
- How are you determining the impact of your work?
- What are you hoping to learn about yourself as a coach?
- What data will you and your coachee bring to the discussion?

Part 2: Questions to Ask and Discuss with Your Coachee

What have you learned about the following:

- Your own leadership and habits of reflection?
- Your school or system?
- The commitment to and evidence of equitable practice within your school or system?

What is an ambitious but realistic vision for success?

- What do you now want to achieve by the end of the coaching engagement? How, if at all, does this differ from your thinking at the start of coaching work?
- What will success look like? How does equity manifest within this vision of success?

What will it take to realize the vision?

- What shifts or changes will be necessary and by whom? What capacity needs to be built for those shifts to be possible?
- What tells you this approach will generate the desired results? Is anything missing?
- What is already in place and can be built on or has been learned thus far?

How will we know if the strategies are working?

- How have we tracked progress thus far? What should we track, monitor, and measure moving forward?

What are the implications for our coaching work?

- What tensions or challenges can we anticipate?
- Are there any changes we should make to how our work together is structured?
- What do we individually and collectively need to start, stop, and continue doing?
- What do we need to (re)commit to for progress to be achieved? How will we hold each other and ourselves accountable?
- What can I do to better support you as a coach?

Phase 4: Reflecting, Celebrating, and Planning Ahead

The final phase of a coaching engagement is all about ending well. By deliberately honing in on the culminating point, you can facilitate a discussion to unpack the impact of the partnership and collaboratively determine what the path is moving forward. This might entail continuing the coaching relationship and refining the approach, or it could involve planning with your coachee for how they will continue to act on and expand their learning after the coaching engagement ends. As was the case with the midpoint, part of winding down a coaching engagement involves:

- Gathering and analyzing data to assess growth and impact, including seeking feedback from the school or broader community.
- Reflecting on the coachee's progress toward coaching goals.
- Identifying the coachee's paradigm and behavioral shifts and potential opportunities for continued growth and development.
- Thinking through what sustaining new practices will entail and what support will be needed.

Here are some key questions you can use to help your coachee plan for sustaining their learning and new practices once your work together comes to an end:

- What is still challenging? What takes deliberate and conscious effort?
- What do you still want or need to do better or more effectively? What else are you interested in learning?
- What will it take for your school or organization to continue cultivating or to sustain a focus on fostering culturally responsive practice?
- What are the implications for you moving forward? How will you hold yourself accountable? What structures/systems can be put in place to support you in following through?

▶ STRUCTURE SESSIONS FOR SUCCESS

Taking a wide perspective allows us to see the entirety of a coaching engagement, but zooming in allows us to hone in on what can take place within a coaching session. As a coach, each question you ask, each piece of feedback you offer, each time you decide whether to keep silent or speak, you are shaping the trajectory of your coaching session. Precisely because you have so much discretion, it can be helpful for you and your coachee to anchor coaching visits in a consistent structure that can support mutual ownership and direction of the coaching relationship.

To that end, The Leadership Academy's (CPR)[2] structure offers a broad outline that coaches and coachees can use together to co-design coaching visits and ensure reciprocal accountability from one session to the next. The six stages of the visit begin with a **Check-In**. This is typically the social dialogue that Clutterbuck describes (see Chapter 5 for more on Clutterbuck's levels of dialogue) – the relationship building, the opportunity to connect and catch up, and also the chance for you as a coach to gauge how your coachee is entering the coaching space – what is their energy like, how are they doing emotionally, and physically.

Once you have checked in, make a **Plan** for the session. Given your coachee's overarching goals and their current context, how do the two of you want to use your time together? You can have a preliminary plan for this, but it will be important to get your coachee's input and agreement to ensure you are collectively invested in how the time will be spent. Next,

Review and connect back to your most recent coaching conversation. Were there any follow-up items for either of you that should be revisited? How does this visit build upon the learning from last time?

Once you have checked in, planned, and reviewed, it's time to **Coach**! Whether you are engaging in a learning walk together, visiting classrooms, role-playing a conversation, debriefing a meeting, or reflecting on feedback, use your skills and the strategies from the previous chapter to maximize learning for your coachee. Then, as you begin to close out the visit, **Procure Commitments** around next steps for you and your coachee. Is there something your coachee will practice before your next session? Is there a resource you will identify and share? Lastly, **Reflect** on the session. Share feedback about the day's conversation with one another.

▶ COACHING SESSION PLANNING TOOL

Before engaging in a coaching session, review your notes and use the questions aligned to the following (CPR)^2 structure to reflect and prepare. We have also included sample question prompts in italics that you can use or customize in your actual coaching meeting.

(CPR)^2 Stage	*Purpose*	*Notes/Questions for Consideration and* Sample Prompts
Connect	Relationship building	What do I know about my coachee that I need to be mindful of when engaging with them? What is happening in their life that I should check in about? • *How are you? How was your day?* • *Anything pressing or top of mind that we need to take care of before we get into the rest of our time together?*

(Continued)

$(CPR)^2$ Stage	Purpose	Notes/Questions for Consideration and Sample Prompts
Plan	Set a goal(s) together for the conversation Plan the session	If this coaching session is successful, how will it help my coachee move toward their intended outcomes? What new learning or insight am I hopeful my coachee will take away? • *What is important for us to achieve today? What do you want to get out of this conversation?* • *From my perspective, I want to (1) better understand XYZ and how that connects to your recent work and then (2) unpack the implications for your leadership and personal development goal. From your perspective, what else do we need to accomplish in this conversation?*
Review	Follow up to last coaching conversation	What did we each commit to at the last session? Have I followed up on the resources or actions I committed to? Based on what they committed to, what opportunities for reflection can I anticipate or prepare? • *We've been working on XYZ... How did it go when you practiced? What did you learn about the work? About yourself?* • *What enabled/got in the way of you completing your commitment?*

(*Continued*)

(CPR)² Stage	Purpose	Notes/Questions for Consideration and Sample Prompts
Coach	Engage in coaching based on agreed-upon goals	Given what I know of my coachee's leadership, style, context, and goals, what might we do, look at, or practice together that would best serve their learning? What are some key questions I want to ask, things I want to listen for or observe? Any feedback I want to provide? Is there any data or evidence I want to examine with my coachee? • *How have you contributed to what we just saw? What role did you play?* • *How do you see your decision in connection with the equity leadership dispositions?* • *What might be the intended and unintended consequences?* • *What would you have done differently? Why?* • *What might be some of your next steps?* • *What conversation(s) do you need to have? With whom?* • *What will be your overarching purpose? What will you say, and how will you say it?* • *What support structures will you put in place?* • *How will you engage others?* • *What's hard about these next steps? What new light does this shed on your leadership?* What can I do ahead of time to ensure my coachee and I are aligned on purpose and to structure the session accordingly (length, time, virtual or in person, etc.)? What emotions may come up for me during the session? How will I respond to or manage these?

(Continued)

(CPR)² Stage	Purpose	Notes/Questions for Consideration and Sample Prompts
Procure Commitment	Determine next steps for both the coach and coachee	How will I cultivate accountability? • *What is important for us to remember from this conversation? How would you summarize the key takeaways?* • *What are our agreed-upon next steps and timeline for follow-up? How can we hold each other accountable? What support do you need from me?*
Reflect	Share feedback	What are my own biases that I need to be conscious of? What can I do to encourage feedback from my coachee? • *What feedback do you have for me?* • *What worked? What could be improved? What can we do differently to make this a better experience?*

▶ GET CLOSE TO THE ACTION

Nothing beats seeing your coachee in action and getting a firsthand sense of their leadership and its impact. Doing so allows you to not just see how others experience your coachee's leadership but also offers you invaluable context to better understand the lens with which your coachee sees themselves, their staff, students, and others within their community. In planning the "Coach" portion of (CPR)², consider the myriad activities you and your coachee could engage in jointly. Here are a few that can be done in person or virtually. Be sure to debrief each experience by sharing low-inference observations, asking questions, and providing feedback.

- Role-play a check-in or post-observation conference with a teacher.

- Shadow your coachee at professional learning sessions, faculty meetings, and informal or formal interactions with staff, students, families, and central office staff. This can be done as a broad observation of their leadership or with a specific lens, such as focusing on something your coachee wants you to look for in their behaviors.
- Talk through a recent interaction with a student's family that was challenging.
- Unpack a recent interaction with a staff member who was feeling overwhelmed or ineffective.
- Support your coachee in designing an agenda for a team meeting or an upcoming professional learning session.
- Look at the curricula being designed by teachers and build your coachee's capacity to provide asset-based and criteria-informed feedback.
- Engage your coachee in conducting a systems-level diagnostic assessment of their school to determine how and where to bring about the most meaningful change. In Appendix E, you will find a School-Level Iceberg Diagnostic tool you can use to engage your coachee and their team in this process.
- Partner with your coachee to conduct a classroom walk-through using The Portrait of a Classroom that is introduced below. You can also find an excerpt from the guide in Appendix D.

THE PORTRAIT OF A CLASSROOM: A CULTURALLY AND LINGUISTICALLY RESPONSIVE CLASSROOM WALKTHROUGH GUIDE

Partnering in a walkthrough is an indispensable opportunity for coach and coachee. By utilizing the Portrait of a Classroom, observers can follow a step-by-step process to determine how to look for culturally and linguistically responsive instruction in schools and create more culturally and linguistically responsive classrooms within a school building. The tool provides guiding questions that are rooted in evidence-based practices for culturally responsive schools, which include Gloria Ladson-Billings' (1994) tenets of culturally relevant pedagogy. The essential elements that leaders must understand and simultaneously attend to are:

- The **academic success** of all students. Culturally responsive leaders center student learning and academic rigor across every school, classroom, and learning environment in their system. They understand and apply college- and career-level standards, select high-quality instructional materials aligned to standards, and hold, model, and communicate consistently high and transparent expectations for all learners.
- The development and deepening of their own **cultural competence** and that of the adults they lead. Culturally responsive leaders affirm the cultures of students and adults through the learning opportunities they provide, the materials they use, the environment they build, and their skill in using cultural understanding to support learning.
- The **cultivation of critical consciousness**. Culturally responsive leaders cultivate and support students' ability to question and critique social norms, values, practices, and systems that produce and maintain inequity.
- **A strong support for the learning, development, and engagement of students from diverse linguistic backgrounds**. Culturally responsive leaders must understand and assess the language needs of multilingual learners and support them in gaining language proficiency.

An excerpt of the tool can be found in Appendix D.

The aforementioned activities represent just a sample of the kinds of experiences that you can design and coordinate with your coachees. It is up to you to determine what would be timely and pertinent to their individual goals, context, and needs.

▶ POST-COACHING SESSION REFLECTION TOOL

Even though your session may be over, your work isn't quite complete. Consider setting aside time after each coaching session to think about your practice, document your coachee's progress, and take note of any immediate next steps or adjustments to make moving forward. Select from the following questions to support your reflections.

- Did we achieve what we wanted to in this session? If not, what happened?
- What new learning or insights did my coachee take away as a result of our work? What will be the impact?
- What did I learn about my coachee? What was confirmed, and/or how will this inform our next interaction?

- What, if any, feedback or questions did I hold back from sharing? Why? What are the implications and/or unintended consequences?
- How did I respond to any biases shared by my coachee?
- Was I triggered at any time during the session? How did I respond? What, if anything, do I need to do differently moving forward?
- What biases showed up for me during the conversation, and how did I respond?
- What feedback did I receive about the conversation? How will this inform my coaching approach moving forward?
- What do I need to learn or do to better support my coachee in developing as a culturally responsive leader?

▶ **FINAL THOUGHTS**

This chapter laid out the importance of coaches being able to adjust their vantage point at pivotal moments to strategically set their coachees up for optimal success and maximum impact. Coaches should be able to adopt a wide-angle lens to see the coaching engagement in its entirety as well as switch to a zoom lens to put an individual session in focus. Toggling back and forth from the "dance floor and the balcony" can be a daunting task, but the tools in this chapter can help you fluidly navigate through a coaching engagement from the first step to the final move.

BACK TO YOU

- What are one to two immediate ways you can take a more action-oriented approach with your coachee? *Try them out in an upcoming coaching session.*
- What changes can you make to the structure of the coaching sessions to maximize impact and transformation? *Utilize the Post-Coaching Session Reflection Tool or make one change in your next coaching session aligned to the (CPR)^2 structure.*
- How can you incorporate a midpoint and culminating discussion to recalibrate coaching or help your coachee sustain practices after the engagement ends? *Use one of the tools or question prompts in this chapter in your next midpoint or culminating coaching session.*
- How can you use walkthroughs to support your coachee in fostering culturally responsive instructional practices? *Try out the Portrait of a Classroom walkthrough guide found in Appendix D.*

Bibliography

Heifetz, R. A., & Linsky, M. (2002). *Leadership on the line: Staying alive through the dangers of change.* Harvard Business Review Press.

Ladson-Billings, G. (1994). *The dreamkeepers: Successful teachers of African American children* (2nd ed.). Jossey-Bass.

Conclusion

> *People oftentimes do not understand the complexity that comes with coaching. They don't understand the deep intrinsic pieces, the nuances, the painstaking deliberation that goes into not just building the relationships but knowing the person and knowing how and what to ask, to prompt them to truly do the work. To me, the most challenging thing about coaching is there is always some uncertainty about how the conversation is going to go. You have to be ready to go where your coachee takes you, and you have to be thinking on your feet.*
>
> – Coach, The Leadership Academy

Every so often, in one of our nationally recognized coach training sessions, someone, especially if they are new to coaching, will ask for things to be more "concrete." They ask questions such as, "Can you tell me specifically when to ask that question." Or they want to know exactly how many coaching sessions to have before bringing up a sensitive topic. The nuance and complexity of the *Facilitative Competency-Based* (FCB) approach to coaching can be daunting. Many tell us that they would feel better if they had clear steps to follow, explicit question stems, session templates, and other resources for guidance. These requests are not surprising. The truth is coaching is hard; it intends to take both the coach and the coachee to their learning edge, and there is no magic formula. It is a dance, co-choreographed by coach and coachee, and if it doesn't feel challenging, there is a good chance you may not be doing it right!

To that end, we hope that this book has not just given you a foundational understanding of what FCB Coaching is all about but also equipped you with plenty of practical tools to bring it to life. In Chapter 1, we laid out the rationale for FCB Coaching and unpacked the actions, skills, and behaviors that comprise this practice. Then, in Chapter 2, we introduced six *Equity Leadership Dispositions* as the underpinning for culturally responsive leadership and described what these look like in action. In Chapters 3–5, we showed you how to operationalize an

FCB approach from the outset of a coaching engagement. We provided a framework for how to set the stage for deeper and more impactful learning, and strategies to keep your coachee in the productive zone of disequilibrium required to achieve meaningful, systemic improvements. Finally, in Chapter 6 and the appendices, we shared a variety of suggested activities and useful structures you can use in your coaching sessions.

Use the tools throughout this book liberally. Try out new techniques with your coachees. Consider the "Back to You" questions and action steps at the end of each chapter to spend a few minutes before and after coaching sessions to reflect on your own practice. Still, you may have come to the end of this book and found that you're longing for even more guidance in helping to develop your FCB Coaching skills. If you or your district need more support, The Leadership Academy can help you. Our website is an online one-stop shop that provides descriptions of our customizable professional learning offerings and services that we can bring to your district, as well as a repository of tools and resources that are regularly updated and refined since we are also continuously learning and improving.

Coaching is more than a skill; it is a leadership stance and FCB Coaching is something you can use daily as you build the capacity of your most precious commodity – your people. While it might be easier to simply tell people what to do based on your experience and expertise, doing so at the exclusion of facilitating their reflection and learning will deny them the opportunities they need to grow into adaptive leaders capable of making transformative change in service of our ultimate beneficiary – the students.

A perfect coach doesn't exist. Effective leadership inherently demands cultural responsiveness. With self-reflection and lots of practice, you can become an accomplished coach who makes a profound difference in the capacity of your coachees. We are confident that you have all you need to get started or to strengthen your skills. That said, coaching is like a dance – there is only so much that you can learn from reading about it. We encourage you to get out there and practice!

Appendix A: Equity Leadership Instrument Excerpt for Reference Only

Note: The following is a small excerpt of a tool developed by The Leadership Academy. Please do not administer it as a survey, as it does not include all items. For further information, please contact research@leadershipacademy.org. This is the introductory language that a leader would see when completing the Equity Leadership Instrument:

To help inform our work together and measure change over time, we ask that you take a few minutes to reflect on the following statements aligned to the leadership dispositions we believe are critical to establishing racially equitable schools and the extent to which they reflect your behavior as an education leader.

Please note: Instead of listing specific groups, the behaviors below use terms such as "marginalized populations," "identity," and "inequities." We are not doing this to mask the specific groups and inequities that exist in our schools – instead, we do not want to limit the groups you consider to the handful that we may list. At The Leadership Academy, we emphasize equity with a focus on race and believe that race intersects with all other inequities, but we recognize that you may be focused on other disparities based on your context.

We encourage you to keep the intersections of identities at the forefront of your mind when reading these behaviors, particularly identities and inequities that may be central to the work in your community. These may include race, sexual orientation, ability, gender, social orientation, socioeconomic status, language, ethnicity, and religion.

We also encourage you to be candid with yourself as you respond to this tool and think about what evidence you might provide for your responses. Leading for equity is an ongoing process. This tool is low-stakes, and your individual responses will not be shared with anyone from your system. The term "system" throughout the instrument refers to whatever system you are helping to lead – this may be a school, district, or some other organization.

Note: The following is a sample of 12 items from the instrument, with 2 items per dimension. The complete instrument has 35 items total, with an average of 6 items for each of the 6 dimensions.

Extent to which these statements reflect your behavior as an education leader:

	Completely	Very Much	Moderately	Slightly	Not at All

Note: The next two items stem from Disposition 1: Reflect on personal beliefs, biases, assumptions, and behaviors.

	Completely	Very Much	Moderately	Slightly	Not at All
I continuously examine and reflect on how my role in the system may contribute to or support inequitable practices.	☐	☐	☐	☐	☐
I identify and continuously examine my assumptions, beliefs, and personal biases.	☐	☐	☐	☐	☐

Note: The next two items stem from Disposition 2: Publicly model a personal belief system that is student-centered and grounded in equity.

	Completely	Very Much	Moderately	Slightly	Not at All
I publicly discuss the work I am doing to become more aware of my own identity, privilege, and biases.	☐	☐	☐	☐	☐
I model vulnerability by acknowledging where there are gaps in my knowledge and skills related to equity.	☐	☐	☐	☐	☐

Note: The next two items stem from Disposition 3: Act with cultural competence and responsiveness in interactions, decision-making, and practice.

	Completely	Very Much	Moderately	Slightly	Not at All
In group discussions, I pay close attention to which voices aren't being heard and invite them to express their perspective.	☐	☐	☐	☐	☐
I actively seek to learn about the identities and communities of students in our school(s).	☐	☐	☐	☐	☐

(Continued)

Note: The next two items stem from Disposition 4: Purposefully build the capacity of others to identify and disrupt inequities in the school.

☐ I ensure that skilled and practiced staff throughout the organization have opportunities to lead conversations around equity.

☐ I design and implement differentiated structures of support, coaching, and professional development to build the capacity of staff to deliver and support culturally responsive instruction.

Note: The next two items stem from Disposition 5: Confront and alter institutional biases of student marginalization, deficit-based schooling, and low expectations associated with race.

☐ I regularly examine data for signs of inequity with my teams or colleagues.

☐ I regularly engage in conversations with stakeholders about racial equity and access, even in the face of risk and pushback.

Note: The next two items stem from Disposition 6: Create equitable systems and structures to promote equity with a focus.

☐ I seek to allocate and manage resources within my sphere of influence to directly support groups that have been historically marginalized.

☐ I work to ensure that issues of equity are incorporated into professional learning opportunities and experiences for all staff.

Appendix B: Goal-Setting Workbook

This tool is intended to help a coach and coachee co-develop their goal(s). It includes the following three stages (Figure B.1):

- The **Preparation Stage** provides some prompts for the coach to consider as they begin planning.
- The **Generation Stage** lays out key elements and sample questions the coach can ask the coachee to initiate their goal-setting discussions.
- The **Inquiry and Analysis Stage** includes questions for both the coach and coachee to explore together as they map out their approach to impact monitoring and measurement.

Lastly, there are additional reflection prompts and questions to surface implications for how the coach and coachee check in and ensure that their relationship is set up for optimal success

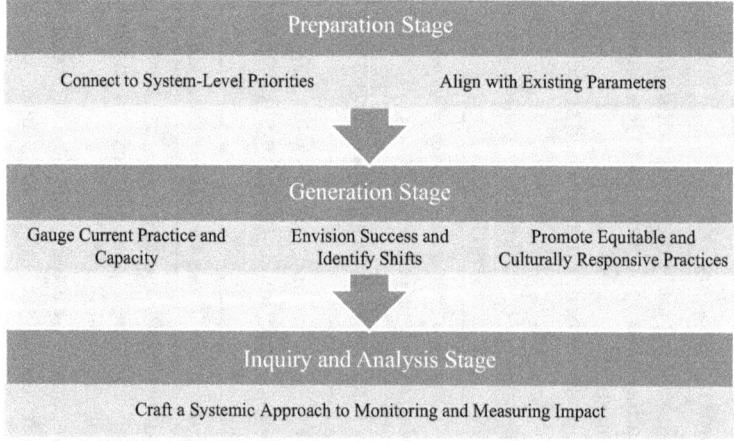

Figure B.1 Three Stages of Goal Setting

▶ PREPARATION STAGE

Connect to system-level priorities: Align goals with the broader organizational context, objectives, and strategic initiatives.

- What is the leader going to be held accountable for in the short and long term?

Align with existing parameters: Ensure that the goals align with the leader's current goal-setting or evaluation system.

- How will the leader be evaluated?
- What leadership framework/model does the system utilize to identify what leaders need to know and be able to do?

▶ GENERATION STAGE

Gauge current practice and capacity: Develop a comprehensive understanding of the leader's current practices and skillset to identify priorities and points of leverage.

- **Questions to ask coachee**:
    - What will making the organizational shifts require of you in terms of your leadership?
    - To what extent are you already exhibiting the necessary leadership actions?
    - In what ways can you leverage your strengths? How might you need to address areas for improvement?

Envision success and identify shifts: Encourage leaders to imagine what goal attainment might look like and identify the mindsets and behaviors that could contribute to and/or hinder advancement.

- **Questions to ask coachee**:
    - Let's imagine 6–12 months from now that you are successful in the things within your sphere of influence and locus of control. What are the three things you have done?

- What are the underlying assumptions at play in terms of how you are thinking about this?
- What mindsets might be getting in your way as you determine a path forward?
- What behaviors would best enable you to make progress toward your goal?
- What might you need to stop, start, and/or continue doing in order to achieve your goals?

Promote equitable and culturally responsive practices: Explicitly mention the intended impact on equitable or culturally responsive practices. Keep students at the center of the work.

- **Questions to ask coachee**:
  - In what ways will students, especially those who have been historically minoritized, benefit?
  - What will be different for children and/or their families if the goal is met?

▶ INQUIRY AND ANALYSIS STAGE

Craft a systematic approach to monitoring and measuring impact: Create a plan to periodically gather evidence, assess progress, and course correct.

- **Questions to explore together**:
  - How will success/impact be defined, and in what ways can it be measured?
  - How will we know that the shifts we are making are reaping the intended benefits for children and families?
  - By what means and in what time frames will we assess progress toward goals? How will we assess the actual versus intended outcomes?

▶ ADDITIONAL REFLECTION PROMPTS AND IMPLICATIONS FOR COACH AND COACHEE

- Is there anything else I (coach) need to know about you (coachee) and your context that I haven't asked? What else, if anything, is essential to ensuring a path toward achievement?

- What are some important milestones during the coaching engagement to set aside for longer coaching conversations?
- How might we keep each other accountable for the work ahead to make progress toward the intended goals? What questions and/or feedback should we give one another if the progress or impact is not being accomplished?

Appendix C: Additional Questions Corresponding to Clutterbuck's Levels of Dialogue

The following are a few examples of questions that a coach can utilize for the various levels of dialogue that may be required during a coaching session. This list is intended to be a starter set. The Leadership Academy cannot emphasize enough that the most effective questions move beyond this stock list and are aligned with a coachee's specific leadership development needs and goals.

Social
Aimed at building and maintaining rapport and trust that underpins effective learning relationships.
• On a scale of 1–4 (1 = drowning, 4 = on top of things), how are you doing right now? • What is top of mind/heart for you? • How have you been feeling lately? What's been bringing you joy or bringing you down? • What can you celebrate today? • How do you recharge your batteries? • What are you looking forward to this (week, month, etc.)? • How are you taking care of yourself?

(*Continued*)

Technical and Tactical
Helps the coachee understand the systems and processes essential to doing a task, as well as work out practical ways to deal with presenting problems or issues they face in their context.
• What are you trying to do/achieve with your staff/team? With your students? • What do you expect to see as a result? How will you communicate those expectations? What will follow-up look like? • What are the steps? What's the timeline? • What is your own understanding/skill level with this? What will you need to learn and do? • Who needs to be involved? Does this require approval? • Who will be the lead facilitator/point person? Who will champion this? • When will they meet? Is coverage needed? • Who has this expertise? Internally and/or externally? • What are the specific skills that need to be developed? What will it look and sound like? • How will this impact the/your classroom? How will it impact students of color (in your school/classroom)? Multilingual learners? Neurodiverse students? • How can the district/school leadership help? • How can you leverage PLCs, grade level meetings, whole faculty meetings, and other professional learning times for your learning and growth? • What resources and/or support are needed? • How will you monitor progress? • What needs to be communicated? To whom?

(*Continued*)

Strategic **Takes the process deeper, providing an opportunity to examine the context and big picture behind an issue and develop longer-term solutions.**
• What are your top priorities/focuses? Why? • What's the reasoning behind your decision/choice? Why is this action step/work important? Why does it matter for your children/class? • How does this align with/intersect with/impact other initiatives? How does this align with the school's instructional focus or improvement plan? • How does this connect to previous work/history? What do you know or can you learn about what happened before? • How did your student/school data inform your priorities? • What is the most important thing that needs to happen? • What conditions do you need to create to ensure success? • Who will join you in this work? Who might be your allies, champions, resistors, and/or challengers? • What is your contingency plan? • What might be some unintended and intended consequences of this action/decision? • What are the costs and benefits? How will you mitigate the costs? How will you maximize the benefits? • What's the next logical step from here? • How will you garner and maintain the resources needed over the long term? • How does this fit into the school schedule? What will need to be changed or shifted? How will you and your team need to use time differently? • How much will and energy does your team and/or the community have for this? • How will you measure success? What could be an early win? • Who does this help, and who does this hurt? • How are you supporting leaders/teachers in unpacking the tenets of culturally responsive pedagogy? • How are you supporting leaders/teachers in ensuring that curricula are culturally and linguistically responsive?

(Continued)

Self-Insight and Behavioral Change
Changes the focus of conversation from the external environment to the internal, builds on these insights, and applies them to support the adoption of new behaviors and actions.
<ul><li>What do you normally do?</li><li>What do you need to do differently?</li><li>Why do you think that is? Why is that important to you?</li><li>What was surprising? What was expected?</li><li>What criteria did you use to make that decision? What data did you consider before making this decision?</li><li>What was your reasoning behind an instructional/leadership decision you made in the moment?</li><li>How did you assess the situation? What didn't you see?</li><li>Is there another way to understand that situation? Another possible explanation? An alternative perspective?</li><li>How might your mental model/bias/assumption have played into your response/action? What role might identity be playing in this situation?</li><li>How are you implicated in the outcomes of your leaders/teachers/students?</li><li>In what ways have you contributed to this issue? What has been your role?</li><li>To what extent are you achieving the result(s) you set out to get?</li><li>What is/was your intent? What are/were you trying to do?</li><li>What was the impact of your action, thought, deed? How did it affect students, families, teachers, other constituents? How did it impact underserved constituents (such as students of color, multilingual learners, students with special needs, and/or those who are neurodiverse)?</li><li>In what ways might you be getting in your own way? How will you correct that?</li><li>What does the school, student, family, teacher, district need from you?</li><li>Why do you feel that way? What's driving your reaction?</li><li>What pattern/trend do you notice in your decision-making/behavior?</li><li>To what extent did your impact align with your intent? How did your decision/action align with your espoused values?</li><li>What's hard about this? Why?</li></ul>

Appendix D: Excerpt of The Leadership Academy's Portrait of a Classroom: *A Culturally and Linguistically Responsive Walkthrough Guide*

The Portrait of a Classroom is a walkthrough tool that can be used as an exercise to understand context, to gather data, and to inform a coaching conversation. It is rooted in Gloria Ladson-Billings' tenets of culturally relevant pedagogy and linguistically responsive instruction that leaders must grasp and address concurrently (To access the full tool, please visit www.leadershipacademy.org).

The process overview: This guide is broken into six distinct steps:

1. Choosing Your Focus Question(s)
2. Leader Self-Reflection
3. The Observation
4. Observation Reflection
5. The Coaching Conversation
6. After the Conversation

Each step is essential, so you are encouraged to use this guide in its entirety. However, we do encourage you to adjust the steps as needed to better align to the needs and current state of your school.

Step one – Choosing your focus question(s): Before you enter a classroom, work with your team to determine the focus of your classroom observations. Choose one or two questions for each visit based on a data analysis, the school's instructional focus area, a problem of practice raised by teachers, or any other data-driven focus for the school. These questions will guide your walkthrough. Given the concern for the safety and security of students in the classroom, be deliberate in providing advance notice to teachers so that they can adequately prepare students for your walkthrough. Teachers and students should know the names of all persons who will be entering the learning environment for the observation and how (or if) members of the observation team may interact with and ask questions of individual students.

Guiding Questions – Academic Success

- In what ways are all students supported in accessing and engaging in work aligned to grade-level and college readiness standards?
- In what ways is the content of the written and actualized lesson aligned to evidence-based best practices and sound curriculum?
- How is the knowledge students bring with them (e.g., language, mobility, neurodiversity, culture) being used as an asset to grow understanding and build upon their funds of knowledge?
- How does the teacher tailor the content, instructional methods, and materials to provide multiple entry points of learning and accountability for a range of students, including those with a disability, multilingual learners, neurodiverse learners, etc.?
- What adjustments have been made to the curriculum and assessments to take into consideration the students' learning strengths, needs, progress in language and literacy development, and neurodiversity? (e.g., timing, seating, scheduling, visual/audio aids, sensory-friendly)
- *If the teacher has set up the classroom so that you have the opportunity to talk directly with a student, ask the student*:
  a. How do you know the teacher believes you can learn this content?
  b. Why is this content important for you to know as a learner?
  c. What would improve your learning experience?
  d. What are the next steps you are going to take in your learning?
  e. How will you know you are successful?

(Continued)

Guiding Questions – Cultural Competence

- How does the teacher show curiosity and appreciation about the intersectionality of their students' lives outside of the classroom and school, including their interests, strengths, and challenges to create grade-level learning experiences?
- How do the students have agency to influence and develop classroom culture?
- How is the classroom environment being used to center students' voices to share, discuss, and challenge one another's thinking?
- How is the text and/or materials used in the classroom inclusive of multiple perspectives and experiences? (e.g., ability, interests, race, class, culture, language, gender identity, neurodiversity)
- How are students encouraged to work collaboratively, fostering peer interactions that value diverse linguistic skills?
- *If the teacher has set up the classroom so that you have the opportunity to talk directly with a student, ask the student*:
  a. How do you get to interact with different classmates in different ways in this classroom?
  b. Do you talk about your race, gender, ethnicity, or other aspects of identity in this class? If yes, what do you get out of these conversations?
  c. Do you feel like you do more listening or more talking while learning in this class?

Guiding Questions – Critical Consciousness

- How are students supported in critically examining and discussing the political, economic, and social forces that shape what and how they learn in alignment with grade-level specific standards?
- How does the teacher encourage and actively support students in identifying and discussing the sociopolitical aspects of their own communities?
- In what ways do teachers provide opportunities for students to build the knowledge, skills, and will to be change agents in the classroom, school, and community?
- How are students encouraged to identify and minimize their own biases across race, language, culture, ability, etc.?
- How are students becoming grade-level appropriate critical assessors of the materials they are utilizing in the classroom?

(*Continued*)

- *If the teacher has set up the classroom so that you have the opportunity to talk directly with a student, ask the student*:
  a. How are you expected to ask questions about your community and the world around you?
  b. How are differing opinions and perspectives appreciated during classroom discussions?
  c. How are you encouraged to critique resources and materials used in the classroom?

Guiding Questions – Linguistically Responsive

Classroom Environment and Linguistic/Cultural Support

- How is the physical classroom environment arranged to support students' diverse linguistic and cultural needs?
- How are teachers integrating culturally and linguistically responsive materials and experiences to connect with students' backgrounds and linguistic needs?
- How do teachers create a linguistically inclusive classroom by affirming home language and culture?

Instruction/Pedagogy

- How do teachers design lessons to meet the diverse needs of multilingual learners?
- What language development strategies do teachers employ to help multilingual students support language proficiency?
- How do teachers create an environment where students have multiple ways to demonstrate their understanding of content as they increase language proficiency?

Monitoring and Assessments

- How does the teacher use formative and summative assessments to analyze content and language progress?
- How does the teacher use assessments to monitor and adjust language acquisition and proficiency?
- How does the teacher use assessments to provide feedback related to language goals?

Step two – Leader self-reflection: In the pursuit of fostering an inclusive and equitable learning environment, it is paramount for school leaders to engage in thoughtful self-reflection regarding their readiness to enhance the cultural and linguistic responsiveness of their teaching staff. Recognizing the dynamic and diverse nature of today's classrooms, leaders must introspectively assess their own understanding of cultural nuances, language diversity, and the unique needs of students from various backgrounds. Before stepping into the role of observing classrooms and providing feedback, school leaders should ponder a series of self-reflection questions.

- Are my own cultural biases influencing my perceptions of effective teaching? If so, how?
- Have I actively sought out professional development opportunities to improve my cultural competency?
    - Which research and evidence-based practices will I leverage to support my observation and coaching?
- Am I well-versed in the cultural backgrounds and languages represented within our student body?
    - What is the ethnic makeup of my school?
    - How many and which languages are spoken by students? Families?
- Do I possess the necessary tools to guide teachers in creating inclusive curricula that honor students' identities and experiences?
    - What local and district resources and tools can I use to support my effectiveness?

By embarking on this journey of self-inquiry, school leaders can better equip themselves to support educators in their pursuit of becoming culturally and linguistically responsive, thereby promoting a more inclusive and empowering educational experience for all students.

Step three – The observation: As you enter the classroom, focus on three key classroom elements: students, teacher, and the content of classroom instruction and discussion. Collect low-inference data and answer the questions at the top of your note-taking tool: "What do you see?" and "What do you hear?" It's also important to make note of the demographics of the teacher and students, for which you can use high inference based on your knowledge of the students and teacher. Talk to students during your observation and ask them what they are doing and why. Give yourself at least 15 minutes in the classroom to gather as much data as possible. If you have a larger group, consider splitting up the focus areas and then bringing your observations together to create a more composite picture.

- Practice:
  - **What do I see? What do I hear?** *Who are the **students** in the room (e.g., race, ethnicity, gender, etc.)?*
  - **What do I see? What do I hear?** *Who is the **teacher** in the room (e.g., race, ethnicity, gender)?*
  - **What do I see? What do I hear?** *What is the **content** being used in the lesson (e.g., standards, curriculum, and instructional materials)?*

Step four – Observation reflection: Once you leave the classroom, take a minute to process what you just saw. Respond to the listed questions on your own before discussing the visit with the others on your walkthrough. You might find that you each notice and focus on different things in the classroom, revealing biases that are important to be cognizant of as you support teachers in building more culturally responsive classrooms. The observation reflection need not take more than 5 minutes and should be done in a location that allows for honest conversation. It is helpful to designate a facilitator for these huddles and to encourage everyone to speak in order to learn from the various perspectives of the group. The observation reflection should happen after each classroom visit. After the second classroom visit, the reflection can focus on trends seen across classrooms.

- Practice:
  - **What am I paying attention to?**
  - **How does my identity play into what I see/what I pay attention to?**

Step five – The coaching conversation. The final important step of a classroom walkthrough is providing feedback to the teacher(s) you observed. Our guide offers sets of questions to help you prepare for, conduct, and reflect on this conversation, helping you frame the initial conversation and think through larger implications for your school. The questions are broken into three sections: before the conversation, the conversation, and after the conversation. The questions are grouped based on the eight action areas outlined in our Portrait of a Culturally Responsive School. Before engaging in a coaching conversation, it is important to review the data you have collected in Step Two and take stock of themes that have emerged. Think about the high-leverage feedback that you can give to the teacher that will help them move closer to creating a culturally and linguistically responsive school. This should all be connected to the focus questions of your walkthrough. This guide provides you with sample questions, but it is not an exhaustive list.

▶ PREPARING FOR THE COACHING CONVERSATION

Self-Reflection Questions for the Coach Prior to the Conversation

Aligned to the Action Area: Lead for Equity and Access

- What biases and blind spots may I bring into the conversation that I need to be conscious of?
- What do I know about this teacher that I need to be mindful of when engaging with them?

Aligned to the Action Area: Strategize Change and Continuous Improvement

- What story is being told from the data I collected?
- What are the themes that emerged from the walkthrough?
- What is the most high- leverage feedback I can give connected to the walkthrough focus question(s)?

▶ CONDUCTING THE COACHING CONVERSATION

Questions for the Coach to Ask the Teacher

Aligned to the Action Area: Focus on Instruction

Academic Success

- What data do you use to plan their lessons?
- How do you make decisions about planned scaffolds? How do you make decisions about in-the-moment scaffolding?
- How are you ensuring that all students are active learners during the lesson?
- How are you using multiple ways of presenting content?
- How can you continue to provide multiple entry points and opportunities for varied assessments in your learning classroom?

Cultural Competence

- How are students able to help shape the classroom?
- How are you creating space in your classroom for students to reflect on their own identities, beliefs, assumptions, and values?
- What high- quality instructional materials are you using that provide students "windows" and "mirrors" of different experiences?
- How are you evaluating curriculum materials for dominant cultural narrative and providing opportunities for students to engage in standards- aligned curriculum?

Critical Consciousness

- How are you creating the classroom environment for students to develop their own critical consciousness?
- How do you overcome biases that may be present in any of the teaching materials, student ideas, etc.?
- How can you continue to provide multiple entry points and opportunities for varied assessments in your classroom?

- How are you supplementing curriculum materials to ensure expansive options are available for students to engage in standards-aligned curriculum?

Linguistic Responsiveness

- How are students able to help shape the classroom?
- How are you designing lessons to meet the diverse needs of multilingual learners?
- How are you using assessments to monitor and adjust language acquisition and proficiency?

Aligned to Other Action Areas

Facilitate Adult Learning and Development

- What are your professional learning goals for this year, and how are they showing up in your daily practice?
- What professional learning is needed as a result of trends seen across classrooms?

Engage in Personal Learning and Development

- How could your mental model or bias have played into your actions in the classroom? Could race be playing a role in this situation?
- What do you need to continue your personal journey to racial consciousness?

Strategize Change and Continuous Improvement

- How are you analyzing data to identify inequities and root causes to make strategic decisions
- What process(es) are in place for evaluating existing school policies, practices, and procedures for cultural and linguistic responsiveness? What prompts you to make changes? What inhibits you from making changes?

Cultivate Community Care and Engagement

- How are you partnering with families to improve the school experience for students?
- Do your families have a comprehensive picture of the academic, social, and emotional standing of their children?

Step six: After the conversation: In this final step of the process, you are reflecting on the coaching conversation. It is critical to take a step away and consider how you explicitly exhibited cultural responsiveness during the conversation and how you can continue to improve your practice. This final step is also the opportunity to document the next steps that will be taken by you and your coachee. Use the guiding questions to take you through this final step.

▶ AFTER THE CONVERSATION (REFLECTION QUESTIONS FOR THE INDIVIDUAL GIVING FEEDBACK)

- How did you respond to any biases shared during the conversation?
- What biases did you exhibit during the conversation?
- What are the agreed upon next steps and timeline for follow-up?
- What support will you be providing after the conversation?
- What feedback did you receive about the conversation?

For access to the full tool, please visit www.leadershipacademy.org.

Appendix E: School Level "Iceberg" Diagnostic Process

The Leadership Academy anchors its work in the tenets of systems thinking, an analytical framework that explores the interconnections between various aspects of a complex system, such as a school. Viewing schools as systems unto themselves and as parts of a larger societal system allows us to understand the dynamic nature of interrelated parts and determine how and where to intervene to influence change (Senge, 1990).

This diagnostic is designed to support coaches, school leaders, and teams in deeply examining key areas of school practice to assess the current state and explore root causes. Adapted from Goodman's (2002) model, "the Iceberg" (Figure E.1) exhibits the layers of inquiry involved in identifying where there are opportunities and leverage for change. For new leaders, this diagnostic is a way to get to know their school context quickly; it is also a way for the leader to engage with the community, elicit multiple perspectives, and utilize different types of data in making initial assessments about the state of the school. The questions are intended to help leaders and teams identify the patterns that underlie presenting issues, the systems and structures that do or do not exist in relation to that data, and the mindsets and behaviors that prevail across the school. To answer the questions, we recommend not just collecting quantitative data but also conducting interviews and focus groups, and observing classroom practices and student and adult behavior.

Once the diagnostic is complete, the coach, the leader, and team identify areas of high impact which become the basis for an action plan that drives the work of the school. The role of the coach is to ensure that the team pays attention to the patterns that

School Level "Iceberg" Diagnostic Process

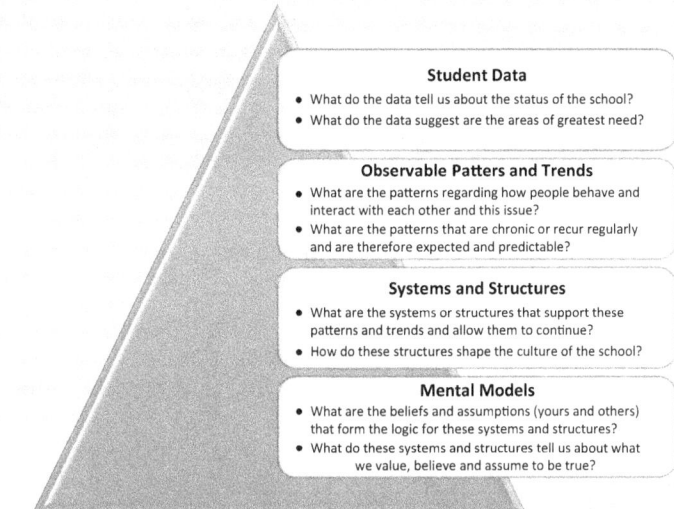

Figure E.1 Iceberg Diagnostic Process

© The Leadership Academy 2024

surface in the diagnostic and crafts an action plan that reflects that diagnosis; additionally, the coach supports the leader and the team in considering implementation challenges, including potential resistance and effective engagement of key stakeholders.

Student Performance and Progress Data
Step 1: Start with a data analysis. Use data from various sources, including student achievement data, demographic data, and cultural and perception data from current and prior years. **Discuss:** What are we seeing in the school data? Which are the most critical findings to investigate?
Observable Patterns and Trends
Step 2: Based on the data analysis, select a handful of questions from the list below or create a set of questions to investigate further. Capture data and evidence through interviews, focus groups, and surveys. Engage in observations of classroom practices and student and adult behavior. • What patterns are evident in classrooms with regard to engagement, participation, and pedagogy?

(Continued)

- How does equity of voice in the classroom manifest through the lens of race, gender, and other identity markers?
- What patterns exist in how teachers implement curricula; in teacher collaboration and inquiry?
- What patterns exist in the way that teachers use data to inform their day-to-day instruction?
- What patterns are evident regarding parental involvement in the school? When do families come to the school? When and how are they invited and greeted? Who attends?
- What are the patterns regarding how multilingual families and families of neurodiverse learners are engaged?
- What are the observable patterns regarding student behavior and discipline?
- What patterns exist as to how students and staff engage with one another in and outside of the classroom? What do interactions look like?
- Who greets students in the morning? What does dismissal look like? What do transitions between classes look like?
- What are the patterns regarding how professional learning is designed, differentiated, and experienced? Who leads, facilitates, and/or provides staff development? Who participates?
- What patterns can be observed regarding how staff collaborate on behalf of students? How do teachers and paraprofessionals work together specifically to address neurodiverse students?
- What are the patterns around how neurodiverse students are identified?
- What are the patterns around how decisions are made throughout the school?

Systems and Structures

Step 3: Explore the patterns that emerged from your analysis: which feel most positive and can be explored more deeply to surface best practices that can be leveraged or replicated? Which patterns feel most critical to disrupt and need further exploration to shift practice? Use the following questions to identify and analyze the systems and structures that lie underneath those patterns of behavior.

- What are the curricula being used? To what extent is it culturally responsive? What routines and rituals facilitate learning across classrooms? How is the curricula used in professional learning?

(Continued)

- What assessments are ongoing and formative? What is the process for designing assessments? How much do assessment processes include multiple ways to represent knowledge and skills and attain outcomes/standards at different points in time? What process does the school use to examine assessments to ensure they are bias-free?
- What formal and informal learning opportunities exist for staff? How are teachers' learning needs assessed? How is the effectiveness of professional development assessed? To what extent, and in what ways, is cultural competence addressed and developed? What support is provided to help teachers understand the culture of the students they serve?
- How does the school schedule support teachers and students? In what ways does it not support them? Who benefits and who does not from the way teachers are assigned?
- What does the improvement process look like for the school? What structures support teacher teaming? What, if any, protocols are in place for team meetings? How do teachers collaborate and share information to support all students?
- How are students grouped – and for what purpose? How are abilities and identity markers considered when forming groups? How are tests modified and evaluated for different students? What biases can be discerned in curricula, tests, and testing formats? How does the school look for and address these?
- What are the formal and informal processes for giving and receiving feedback among different stakeholders? (Teachers, students, parents, and families)
- What are the processes for recruitment? To what extent are they successful in yielding a diverse staff? What structures are used to eliminate bias in hiring practices?
- What data or goals inform how resources are apportioned? Who benefits and who does not benefit from the ways in which resources are allocated?
- What structures and resources support low-performing students and students with learning differences? What does the intervention process look like, and who owns it? How do students move in and out of the process?
- How is information about student behavior and socio-emotional needs shared with teachers, staff, and families?
- How does the physical layout inform school culture? Where are the classrooms for neurodiverse students located?

(Continued)

- What are the key points of contact with parents and community members? How are non-English speakers accommodated? Which school signs, letters home, and other pieces of communication are written in the major languages spoken by parents and students?
- What are the school structures that support wellness and health? Career and college readiness? How are they being utilized? What gaps exist, and for whom?
- What are the policies and procedures around student behavior? What professional learning is provided for teachers around managing student behavior?
- What rituals and routines hold meaning for students? In what ways do extracurricular activities reflect and affirm the cultures, identities, histories, or interests of students?
- Who is considered part of the cabinet and the leadership team? What is the purpose of their meetings? How often do they occur? How are decisions made and communicated? What information is shared and how? How does the cabinet and leadership team distribute roles, responsibilities, and tasks? What is the accountability structure for the team? What kind of data do the teams collect and monitor?
- What official and unofficial power structures can be discerned within the school community? How diverse are they? Where are the gaps in representation?

Mental Models

Step 4: Consider what has been learned from delving into the structures or lack of structures that uphold the patterns you have identified. What are the beliefs, values, assumptions, and mental models that undergird those structures? Use the following questions to identify the mental models and beliefs at play in the school that inhibit student success and keep inequitable practices in place.

- What is considered "success" at the school, and how is it celebrated?
- What do staff and leaders believe about equity and culturally responsive practice as it pertains to the school?
- What belief systems are discernable in the community about members from different racial, ethnic and cultural backgrounds?

(Continued)

- What do staff and leaders expect (and not expect) from students? How does this differ across lines of identity? What biases or bias-based beliefs are evident?
- What are the espoused and enacted beliefs about students and behavior? How does this differ across lines of identity?
- What are the staff and leader's beliefs about who is accountable for the students' learning?
- What are core beliefs about how good teaching happens? What "rigor" looks like?
- What are the school's espoused and enacted beliefs about how to best serve neurodiverse students and multilingual students or English language learners? What expectations do staff have for those students?
- What are the beliefs around what good professional learning and development looks like?
- What are some of the belief systems about the role of parents in the school and about the role parents play in their children's education? How does this differ across lines of identity?

Bibliography

Baumer, N., & Frueh, J. (November 23, 2021). What is neurodiversity. *Mind and mood.* Harvard Health Publishing. https://www.health.harvard.edu/blog/what-is-neurodiversity-202111232645

Goodman, M. (2002). *The Iceberg model.* Innovation Associates Organizational Learning.

Murphy, J. (2007). Restructuring through learning-focused leadership. In H. Walberg (Ed.), *Handbook on restructuring and substantial school improvement.* Center on Innovation and Improvement.

Senge, P. (1990). *The fifth discipline: The art and practice of the learning organization.* Doubleday/Currency.

Spiro, J. (2011). *Leading change step-by-step: Tactics, tools, and tales.* Jossey-Bass.

Glossary

Active listening is defined as both a willingness and an ability to hear and understand others. It's portrayed as a dynamic exchange where conversations are enhanced when one person engages in active listening (Hoppe, 2007).

Adaptive leadership is the practice of mobilizing people to take on tough challenges and thrive. It is distinguished from technical work, for which there are known solutions (Heifetz, 1989).

Cognitive dissonance is a psychological phenomenon that occurs when a person holds two or more contradictory beliefs or values, or when their behavior does not align with their beliefs or values (Kumar-Lanka, 2018).

Container signifies a symbolic and emotional space or environment where the coaching interaction unfolds.

Culturally responsive leader is a leader who recognizes the impact of institutionalized racism on their own lives and the lives of the students and families they work with and embraces their role in mitigating, disrupting, and dismantling systemic oppression.

Directive coaching is a style of coaching that builds one's knowledge and skill set through teaching, providing guidance and suggestions, and directly sharing new ideas (Bloom, 2005).

Equity means every school and school system is intentionally built to ensure children of every race, ethnicity, language or other characteristics of their identity, have what they need to achieve academic, social, and emotional success.

Facilitative coaching is a coaching style that builds one's reflective practice. Facilitative coaching builds on the coachee's existing knowledge and skills to form new learning, beliefs, and behaviors (Bloom, 2005).

Facilitative competency-based coaching (FCB) is a job-embedded iterative approach to school and system leadership development in which two people (coach and coachee) work together around an agreed upon set of skills, knowledge, and behaviors (competencies).

Fixed mindset is a belief that one's basic qualities, like intelligence or talent, are immutable traits that cannot be grown (Dweck, 2006).

Growth mindset is coined by Carol Dweck (Dweck, 2006) and is a way of thinking that involves recognizing that challenges, setbacks, and discomfort are not obstacles but rather opportunities for learning and personal growth. Adults who believe in their capacity to develop and learn are more likely to engage in challenging tasks, take risks, and embrace discomfort as a means of expanding their capabilities.

Holding environment is a space where the coachee feels safe and can examine and interact with his/her inner and outer worlds. A good holding environment meets a person's needs by recognizing and confirming who that person is and how he or she makes meaning. It also challenges the coachee to grow beyond his or her existing perceptions to new and greater ways of knowing (Kegan, 1994).

Ladder of inference is a model that helps individuals understand and analyze their thought processes and how they form beliefs and make decisions (Senge, 2006).

Leadership competencies are the knowledge, skills, and dispositions necessary to be an effective leader. The Leadership Academy believes that coaching is most effective when it is anchored in a standards-aligned, contextually relevant competency framework that identifies what leaders need to know and be able to do to raise academic, social, and emotional success for all students.

Learning edge is the area or pathway for future growth and development.

Limiting assumptions are core beliefs one has about the world or himself/herself that prevent one from developing as completely as one would like.

Low-inference data is observable data expressed in a nonjudgmental way. Documenting what one sees and hears. It disciplines participants in the examination of facts that are rooted in what is actually happening (Texas Education Agency).

Example:

Low inference: Teacher used SmartBoard to work through the word problem

High inference: Teacher makes good use of technology

Mental models   refer to the deeply ingrained assumptions, generalizations, or images that influence how we understand the world and how we take action. In coaching, and more broadly in disciplines such as organizational learning and systems thinking, "mental models" are the internal constructs of our mind that we use to make sense of our experiences. They may loosely be referred to as our prejudgments. They serve as a filter that determines what we actually see and shapes how we act (Senge, 2006).

Minoritized   emphasizes what the school systems and other systems within the United States have overtly and covertly done to Asian, Black, Indigenous, Latinx and Students of Color. The term was coined by Michael Benitez, Jr., to refer to the "history of structural and institutional actions that have over time limited access to and led to a lack of presence among students of color in higher education labeled as racially and ethnically different from the norm." The term is meant to build a "more critical understanding of how 'minority' came to be constructed socially over the course of history and how students continue to be minoritized in contemporary spaces of higher education."

Neurodiversity   "describes the idea that people experience and interact with the world around them in many different ways; there is no one 'right' way of thinking, learning, and behaving, and differences are not viewed as deficits" (Baumer & Frueh, 2021).

Productive zone of disequilibrium (PZD)   is the optimal range of distress within which the urgency in the system motivates people to engage in adaptive work. If the level is too low, people will be inclined to complacently maintain their current way of working, but if it is too high, people are likely to be overwhelmed and may start to panic or engage in severe forms of work avoidance (Heifetz et al., 2009).

Racial identity   is a sense of group or collective identity based on one's perception that he or she shares a common racial heritage with a particular racial group (Helms, 1990; Daniel Tatum, 1992).

Bibliography

Baumer, N., & Frueh, J. (November 23, 2021). What is neurodiversity. *Mind and mood.* Harvard Health Publishing. https://www.health.harvard.edu/blog/what-is-neurodiversity-202111232645

Bloom, G. (2005). *Blended coaching: Skills and strategies to support principal development.* Corwin Press.

Dweck, C. (2006). *Mindset: The new psychology of success* [Kindle version]. Ballantine Books.

Heifetz, Ronald A. (1989). *Leadership without Easy Answers.* Harvard University Press.

Heifetz, R. A., Grashow, A., & Linsky, M. (2009). *The practice of adaptive leadership: Tools and tactics for changing your organization and the world.* Harvard Business Press.

Helms, J. (1990). *Black and white racial identity: Theory, research and practice.* Greenwood Press.

Hoppe, Michael. (2007). Lending an ear: Why leaders must learn to listen actively. *Leadership in Action, 27*(4), 11–14.

Kegan, R. (1994). *In over our heads: The mental demands of modern life.* Harvard University Press.

Kumar-Lanka, Vijaya. (September 20, 2018). Coaching agile teams through cognitive dissonance. *LinkedIn Blog.* https://www.linkedin.com/pulse/coaching-agile-teams-through-cognitive-dissonance-vijaya-kumar-lanka/

Senge, P. (2006). *The fifth discipline.* Random House Business.

Tatum, Beverly Daniel. (1992). Talking about race, learning about racism: The application of racial identity development theory in the classroom. *Harvard Educational Review, 62*(1), 1–24.

For Product Safety Concerns and Information please contact our EU
representative GPSR@taylorandfrancis.com
Taylor & Francis Verlag GmbH, Kaufingerstraße 24, 80331 München, Germany

www.ingramcontent.com/pod-product-compliance
Lightning Source LLC
Chambersburg PA
CBHW052341230426
43664CB00041B/2598